THE EARTHBOUND PARENT

THE EARTHBOUND PARENT

*How (and Why) to Raise
Your Little Angels Without Religion*

RICHARD A. CONN, JR.

Foreword by Robyn E. Blumner

PITCHSTONE PUBLISHING
Durham, North Carolina

Pitchstone Publishing
Durham, North Carolina
www.pitchstonepublishing.com

10 9 8 7 6 5 4 3 2 1

Library of Congress Cataloging-in-Publication Data

Names: Conn, Richard A., author.
Title: The earthbound parent : how (and why) to raise your little angels
   without religion / Richard A. Conn, Jr. ; foreword by Robyn E. Blumner.
Description: Durham, North Carolina : Pitchstone Publishing, 2018. | Includes
   bibliographical references.
Identifiers: LCCN 2017058148 (print) | LCCN 2018003853 (ebook) | ISBN
   9781634311632 (epub) | ISBN 9781634311649 (ePDF) | ISBN 9781634311656 (
   mobi) | ISBN 9781634311625 (pbk. : alk. paper)
Subjects: LCSH: Parenting—Religious aspects. | Child rearing—Religious
   aspects. | Irreligion.
Classification: LCC BL625.8 (ebook) | LCC BL625.8 .C66 2018 (print) | DDC
   649/.7—dc23
LC record available at https://lccn.loc.gov/2017058148

To my own little angels:
Jordan, Dylan, Nikita and Natalie,
whom I love so much and who provide immeasurable
and constant joy to their parents

Our planet is a lonely speck in the great enveloping cosmic dark. In our obscurity, in all this vastness, there is no hint that help will come from elsewhere to save us from ourselves.

—Carl Sagan, *Pale Blue Dot*

CONTENTS

Foreword by Robyn E. Blumner   11

Preface   15

Acknowledgments   19

Introduction   23

1. Life in the Cave: Seeing the Shadows on the Wall   27

2. The Desire for a Savior: Understanding Our Fears and Desires   31

3. The Journey Out of the Cave: Finding a Path with Critical Thinking   59

4. The Nature of Morality: Being Good Without God   75

5. Life under the Sun: Embracing the Benefits of Abandoning Religion   83

6. The Earthbound Parent: Raising Good Children Without Religion   95

Conclusion   135

Appendix: Answers to Common Questions   139

Chapter Notes   145

FOREWORD

Want to raise smart, grounded, and moral children, fully equipped to navigate the world and flourish on their own terms? Richard A. Conn, Jr. tells you how. In this much-needed and timely volume, he shares his proven recipe—tested and refined over decades in his own home with his four children. It includes lots of commonsense ingredients, such as loving hugs, solid role models, exposure to a variety of cultures and foreign languages, and minimal television, but here's the real key: no religion added.

Informed not only by his long-standing experience as a father but also by his considerable international experience as a lawyer, consultant, and investor, Conn underwrites a strong alternative to religion for raising children. He endorses a humane, caring, and responsible attitude toward others and the world while rejecting what he calls "nihilism." In so doing, he presents a set of eminently reasonable precepts, guidelines, and suggestions for ethical but secular child rearing, showing how to ensure that children internalize moral values without the fear of a supernatural threat. In this regard, *The Earthbound Parent* offers a gentler and more instructive version of Richard Dawkins' oft-cited (and to my mind, accurate) view that raising children with a fear of eternal damnation is a form of child abuse.

Unlike many other parenting guides, *The Earthbound Parent* is, by design, as much a how-to as a why-to. Thus, Conn writes not only for those parents who have abandoned religion altogether—or who never had it to begin with—but also for those who often find themselves sitting uncomfortably in the pews. While acknowledging that religion can provide solace and other tangible benefits, he touches on the all-too-familiar ways that religion can justify hostile attitudes, shocking discrimination, and violent actions—all while inhibiting critical thinking, scientific discovery, and practical reason-based government policies. By calling on parents to resist the temptation to succumb to inertia or simple habit when deciding how or when to introduce religion, he advocates not only for the benefit of children but also for the advancement of society as a whole.

Yet, Conn understands the difficulty many parents face when determining whether to raise their children without religion and covers the intellectual, emotional, and practical elements parents must consider in making this crucial decision. While he aims to persuade the reader of the net harm caused by religion on both a micro and macro level, he does not demean those who have faith. Still, for those parents who themselves identify as religious, his recommendations are perhaps best suited for the ones who think bromides such as "thoughts and prayers" are never a substitute for reasoned action and change. And for those parents who see the benefit of raising their children in a secular manner but fear losing beloved traditions, he advises that raising children without religious faith need not mean completely detaching them from the family's cultural touchstones or heritage. I'm reminded here of comedian Sarah Silverman's joke about her own religio-cultural identity as a Jewish atheist: "I'm Jewish, but I'm totally not."

Conn's insightful text will be, dare I say it, a revelation to many parents who want to raise their children to be happy and successful but who have been socialized to believe that religion is a necessary part of that formula. He both exposes the deleterious effects of supernatural beliefs and proposes a path forward without them. The ideas he presents deserve to be considered by all who care about the arc of civilization; collectively, they trace an effective approach for reducing religious influence and its worst excesses in our society and politics.

The Earthbound Parent is thus not only informational but also aspirational. Indeed, its aim reflects Richard Dawkins' observation that religion, like almost every other aspect of culture, depends on its intergenerational transmission for survival. And just as genes are subjected to selective pressure, so too are cultural ideas. However, the needed pressure to curb or inhibit the transmission of harmful religious beliefs will not occur in isolation; thus, we all have an obligation to apply our own form of pressure.

Only through collective cooperative behavior can we create meaningful change in the face of long-entrenched religious faith and dogma. Conn, for his part, is fulfilling his own obligation in how he is rearing his children. And now, through this book, he calls on other parents to do the same, so that all children—present and future—will cease learning that human life is nothing more than a trial run for some future heavenly (or hellish) one. After all, humankind is a social species, and we will be unable to solve our most-pressing worldly problems—whether as individuals or a global society—if we continue to teach children that seeking answers from an imaginary figure in the sky has more value than working toward reality-based solutions here on Earth.

Robyn E. Blumner
President & CEO, Center for Inquiry
Executive Director, Richard Dawkins Foundation
for Reason & Science

PREFACE

This book encourages you to raise your children without religion or religious belief of any kind. It maintains that a belief in god or gods is a delusional state of mind—just as delusional a state of mind as a belief in Santa Claus, the Easter Bunny, or an imaginary friend—and it maintains that delusional states of mind are dangerous for both individuals and societies. It contends that we should not hold beliefs merely because they calm our fears or gratify our desires or because our ancestors held certain supernatural beliefs that have been passed along through the ages, that we should remain agnostic about things for which we have no evidence, and that the dogmatism that religions support is dangerous for both individuals and societies. It explains a thought process that leads away from religion and toward critical thinking. Moreover, it constitutes an argument against passing along religious doctrines to our children and offers practical suggestions on how to raise children without religion.

I approach the subject as a parent who wants the best for my kids—I have four of my own plus two grandchildren. I care deeply about imparting proper values to them and helping all children challenge assumptions, reason for themselves, and develop confidence in their own judgment.

What do I mean by saying religious views are "delusional"? I use the term in the commonsense manner, as defined, for example, in Wikipedia ("a belief held with strong conviction despite superior evidence to the contrary") and the Collins Dictionary ("a belief held in the face of evidence to the contrary, that is resistant to all reason").

I have no doubt that many of you will find my criticisms of religion and my prescriptions for parenting upsetting. Everyone is entitled to believe whatever they wish and I realize that most of the world is religious. I am not advocating banning religion or vilifying those who hold religious beliefs. Rather, I seek to help inoculate children against such beliefs. A child's innocent belief in Santa Claus will not result in the killing of people, but an adult's extremist belief in a God or gods can. The battle over who has the best imaginary friend has led to the butchering of countless people throughout recorded history and remains a root cause of horrific violence today, both on the individual and societal level. If you agree with me that people killing one another is a thing to be prevented however possible, then perhaps you will allow me to explore with you a first step toward ending religiously motivated violence and conflict.

You may be raising your child in an environment where critical thinking in the realm of religion is strongly discouraged or even punished. You may worry that if you raise your child without religion and religious beliefs, she will grow up without moral values, ethical principles, appropriate standards of conduct, and the ability to distinguish between what is right and wrong. You may sense a conflict between your desire to encourage your child to learn how to think for herself and make judgments of her own, and your religious culture's insistence upon uncritical obedience and "faith." Or you may believe that raising your child to be a critical thinker will only result in her ostracism from polite society, or her condemnation to hell, or some other natural or supernatural punishment.

This book responds to the above-mentioned worries as well as to many others that caring parents may have. Designed to be a stand-alone, relatively simple, concise yet comprehensive work, it encompasses concepts, practical tips, and the thinking of other authors when and where relevant. Whether or not you choose to raise your child without religion, I hope that the perspectives this book offers will convince you that there are alternatives to religious indoctrination and that they do not lead inexorably to a life without values or meaning. I hope that the book will persuade you that people can lead meaningful, peaceful, and productive lives without believing in a god, or indeed relying upon any other kind of supernatural being to explain existence and give a purpose to life. And I hope that, whether you are slightly religious, very religious, or somewhere in between on the religious spectrum, you will be left with fewer reasons than you currently have to demonize those who do not believe in your god—or, indeed, in any supernatural spirit at all.

I do not find it hard to imagine (to paraphrase John Lennon's "Imagine") that there is no religion: no heaven above, no hell below, and no god to send us to either one. Indeed, I find it difficult to imagine it any other way. I can easily imagine how ancient people may have needed a god or gods to explain the world they found around them. Why would a peaceful blue sky suddenly darken into a terrifying thunder and lightning storm? Why is there something rather than nothing? Why do we exist at all? What happens to us after we die?

A belief in supernatural forces (gods) seems to me to be so primitive that I find it hard to understand how people, and especially educated people, can still hold it today. How can we cleave to religious belief systems that have led, and continue to lead, to so much fear, hatred, war, death, and destruction in the world? The costs of religion at our current stage of civilization outweigh the benefits. This book explores why we cling to religion in the face of overwhelming reason to reject it.

This is not just a "why-to" book, however; it is also a "how-to" book that is intended to describe how you can, and why you should, raise your children without indoctrinating them into religious belief systems that have led to all that fear, hatred, war, death, and destruction—in short, so they might understand that we are bound on this Earth together and recognize that we have only ourselves on which to rely.

ACKNOWLEDGMENTS

I would like to thank my friends who read and commented on various drafts of the book, albeit without attribution at their request due to the nature of the book's subject matter. Special thanks go to Alex Rosenberg for connecting me to Richard Dawkins; Richard Dawkins for providing me with timely encouragement and an introduction to his foundation; Kurt Volkan for making this happen as publisher; and Julianna, my lovely wife, for her gentle mixture of insouciance and support in whatever I undertake.

THE EARTHBOUND PARENT

INTRODUCTION

Our place in the universe and our role as parents are closely related, because how we see our place in the universe will invariably affect our parenting decisions. If, for example, we believe that we are the offspring of a deity that controls the universe, then we will likely pass this perspective along to our children through both word and action. Similarly, an understanding of our place in the universe that includes no God, gods, or other supernatural forces will typically result in nonreligious parenting—or, as I refer to it, Earthbound parenting, a recognition that we should, to paraphrase Carl Sagan, recognize the folly of human conceit, deal more kindly with one another, and preserve and cherish what we have here on Earth.

As I argue, we should all embrace both a nonreligious understanding of our place in the universe and, along with it, nonreligious ways to raise our children. I did this with my first two children years ago and I am doing it again with my second generation of children now. Some of my parental choices may seem odd to you. Just as my kids have had no exposure to television in our home, so too have they had no exposure to religion. I have, however, encouraged them to participate in sports, pick up an instrument, learn foreign languages, appreciate the arts, play chess, and, yes, even watch select programing on the Internet.

How can a caring parent raise a child without religion? This book explains how to do it and why doing so makes sense. All parents must decide for themselves which traditions to pass along to their children and which traditions to cast aside or alter. I chose not to pass along my family's religious traditions. I want to explain why I did so and to encourage you to consider doing the same.

This book maintains that the world would be better off without religion and that one way forward is for parents to take responsibility for making and implementing the decision not to pass on their religious traditions as they raise their children. But our religious fantasies are so deeply entrenched in our societies and in our minds that rooting them out entirely would present a seemingly impossible challenge even if we all agreed a religion-free world would be an improvement. This book is accordingly written for religious and nonreligious parents alike who may wonder whether passing religion on to their children is really in the best interests of their children and the world.

I hope you will find my reasons compelling and conclude as I did that the pluses outweigh the minuses. I hope that the cumulative effect of parents deciding not to pass on their religious traditions to their children will benefit not only their own families, but society as well. Be this as it may, I believe that the advancement of civilization depends, at least in part, upon individual parents making the choice to forgo religious training in raising their children in an attempt to leave behind the ancient myths that have divided our societies and fostered conflict among them.

This book presents a philosophical argument in favor of a life without religion for you to weigh against the vast historical, literary, political, and cultural forces aligned in favor of a life with religion. I repeat, it is not meant to cause offense or to suggest that religion be banned. But it is meant to persuade you, and may therefore advocate perspectives that you may disagree with.

The first and second chapters of this book will give reasons for seeing yourself in a nonreligious universe. I will first present evidence about our physical location in the universe and about our constituent elements, and I will propose that these facts do not fit standard religious narratives. I do not intend this evidence to prove that God does not exist—I do not believe that such a proof is possible—but only to show the tremendous implausibility of a god or gods and to invite you to doubt the foundational idea of religious belief. I will then discuss the psychological forces that drive us toward a belief in religion and religion's numerous conflicts with science and reason. And I will do this for much the same purpose, namely to cause you to question your own motivations for embracing religion. The combination of these two factors— our physical location and our psychological proclivities—led me to conclude years ago that it is highly unlikely that religion is anything but nonsense.

In the third chapter I present an escape plan from the labyrinth of religion. The path focuses upon utilizing critical thinking to help you disengage from the cycle of passing along belief in the supernatural to the next generation.

The fourth chapter of the book addresses how this conclusion about religion affects the child-rearing choices that parents must make. I examine the purported necessity of religion for morality— this is the question I hear most frequently from other parents— and I describe how children can become well-adapted moral adults without it. I contend, once again, that religious belief is a delusion that should be identified as such by parents, and that halting its transmission from parents to children is in the best interest of both the child and society.

In the fifth chapter I explore some of the positive effects that raising children without religion may have upon society. What would take the place of religious belief if we did not teach it? How would we instill values and provide community? I argue that natural maternal and paternal instincts combined with existing legal and social structures are excellent alternatives.

Finally, in the sixth chapter I move from why parents should raise their children without religion to how they should do so. While some of my general parenting tips may be of interest to parents who are raising their children to embrace religion, most of the section focuses on secular parenting tips. Of course, just as you as the parent will decide whether to raise your children without religion, you will also decide how to go about doing so. This last section should give you some useful ideas to ponder.

Our individual parenting decisions may not seem important in the broader context, but cumulatively they matter a great deal. We create the possibility of chipping away at the toxic mixture of politics and religion that continues to dominate our lives. I suggest that religion stands in the way of a more peaceful world by depriving us of the power of reason and tolerance. As an example, consider our ongoing response to religiously fueled terrorism. While military might and a solid defense are clearly the short-term solutions to terrorism, the longer-term solution requires identifying the problem—including, notably, delusional thinking centered upon religion—followed by the gradual marginalization of such "thinking." Accordingly, the answer ultimately lies in individual homes, where we make decisions about how we view religion and the level of respect we should accord it. Only after we see the delusions in our own beliefs and lives can we begin to educate and persuade others about the dangers of religion.

But, as things stand today, our hands are tied, because we in the West have our own time-honored and well-entrenched religious delusions. We share the same basic paradigm that has long been one of the engines of religious terrorism, violence, and abuses. So rather than condemning the beliefs of religious extremists as delusional and promoting reason as their proper antidote, we actually uphold their religion and argue that they have simply misinterpreted it. Why do we do this? Because we cannot assert that their religious beliefs are delusional without simultaneously admitting that our own religious beliefs are delusional too.

This book, I hope, will help to solve this problem.

1

LIFE IN THE CAVE

Seeing the Shadows on the Wall

Plato used to tell a story about people who unknowingly lived their lives imprisoned in a cave. With their feet chained to a bench, and immobile from the neck up, these people were unable to turn their heads to see the great fire burning far behind them. They could instead see only the shadows of the animals and people that passed by it on the wall in front of them. Unaware that the shapes were even shadows, they readily mistook them for reality itself and developed a system of beliefs based upon them. Plato's point was that we ourselves are not all that different from the prisoners in his cave—that we are all raised to accept certain "truths" and to hold certain beliefs that may be nothing more than shadows on a wall.

Many of you might have seen—or perhaps even still see—the shadows I once saw. My parents told me when I was very young that I am part of a special group of people who had been created by a powerful god that looks and thinks very much like a human being. They told me that each member of this group is special, unique, and, indeed, chosen. They told me that this god watches over what we do, that he punishes us for doing bad and rewards us for doing good, and that he is responsible for creating and maintaining everything else that exists. They told me that the god has always existed, that it still exists, and that it will always exist; that it observes us constantly and can read our thoughts; that it wants our obedience, our attention, our gratitude, and our worship; and that it will reward us in various ways both during our lifetimes and after our deaths—if, that is, we meet its expectations. They told me, in fact, that part of this reward is that we will never really die and that some central essence of us will be preserved forever in a wonderful place called heaven. The details may differ here and there, but this is probably not all that far off from what your parents told you.

But now let's consider what my parents did not tell me about the shadows on the wall—that I am physically located on a relatively small planet that is orbiting a relatively small star that is floating in an ocean of space that is a trillion times larger than anything I can conceive. Nor did they tell me that I am constructed from stardust that has been organized by genetic codes that evolved over billions of years. But as I studied the basics of modern science, I came to see my physical location in the universe as inconsistent with the grand role that humanity purportedly plays in god's drama. Since the time of Copernicus and Galileo, our physical location has been beyond dispute. The constituent elements of our bodies are too, and they are undeniably commonplace. One may, of course, always argue that these elements were themselves created by a god. But modern science makes it harder and harder with each passing year to believe that we need to appeal to a supernatural god to explain our existence and place in the universe—or anything else for that matter.

I had a huge advantage in rejecting religion over those born before 1859. Why so? Because prior to 1859, we lacked Darwin's scientific explanation of how humans came to exist.

The concept of natural selection dates back to at least Empedocles (400 BCE) and Lucretius (99–55 BCE). But Darwin was the first to develop this concept and link it to the creation of new species. The publication of *On the Origin of Species* provided us with an alternative explanation to the god story. Darwin's explanation fit the available evidence and did not require a supernatural cause. It thus undermined the need to appeal to a god to explain our existence. Religious belief began to shrink as modern science continued to explain things we previously could not explain without appealing to a god. I believe that each new generation will find it easier to reject religion as science continues to explain more and more about the world around us.

Science undermines the need for religion by providing answers to questions that religion used to answer before we found better ones. We could talk about gods living on mountaintops until we climbed to the tops of mountains and found no gods living there. We could talk about gods living in the clouds until airplanes took us to the clouds and we found no gods living there. It became more and more difficult to talk about a hell below us once geological science made it clear that Earth is round and solid with a core and not hollow with an underworld. We travel in space and see great distances through our telescopes yet we have not found gods or heaven. Religions are now less specific about exactly where they are supposed to be located.

My point is very simple. It is that an objective analysis of our physical location and makeup simply does not support the idea that we are particularly special, or chosen, let alone created by a god. Our planet occupies a place of profound insignificance in a vast universe. This is the physical reality of our location. And it is a daunting task to find significance in our lives, or to feel special, or chosen, if we accept the fact that we occupy such a tiny place in the universe. It was easier to feel special or chosen thousands of years ago when most of our religions and religious beliefs were formed.

Science as we know it did not yet exist. No one knew our physical place in the universe. So it was easy to believe that we were the center of the universe and of special interest to a supernatural divine creator. Now it is more difficult to link our physical reality with a belief that we are at the center of anything.

In many highly religious societies, education is focused on religious doctrine so religion's conflict with science does not become apparent. Even in moderately religious societies, children are indoctrinated with a powerful religious narrative before they reach the age of reason. What are the chances this sort of religious narrative, passed sacredly from one generation to the next, would last in a society if it were communicated only to adults? Today's scientific knowledge stands too firmly in the way of such highly unlikely religious myths. Any adult with the most basic knowledge about the world would be skeptical of the many far-fetched stories that serve as the foundation of religions if they were told for the first time today. It is only the age of religions themselves, our collective cultural indoctrination, and, in much of the world, certain legal protections that bar the full exposure of religions. Indeed, in some societies today, challenging religious ideas risks severe punishment—even death.

But something keeps many adults from confronting the patent inconsistencies of religious teaching. Even in the face of Darwinism and ever-mounting scientific evidence explaining virtually everything in our lives and experiences, there is still something that drives people toward religion. What causes so many people to build their lives around delusional beliefs and myths beyond the fact that they are passed down by trusted parents and elders? Put simply, religion is a form of fantasy or, more precisely, a form of self-deception—or even denial—that we are attracted to for powerful psychological and societal reasons.

2

THE DESIRE FOR A SAVIOR

Understanding Our Fears and Desires

Ever since the dawn of religion, people have focused on whatever god happened to be in vogue at the time. Christopher Hitchens' book *God Is Not Great: How Religion Poisons Everything* contains a long list of gods that humans have worshipped throughout history, virtually all of which have now faded into oblivion. From Egyptian Sun worship through Judaism, and from Judaism through Christianity, Islam, and their various present-day derivations, gods have always been portrayed as keenly interested in human affairs. Greek and Roman Mythology is replete with tales of gods watching over us and taking part in the affairs of humans: talking with humans, siring children with humans, posing tests and quests for humans, taking sides in wars fought by humans, answering the prayers of humans, etc. The Bible is replete with such stories too. The Bible teaches that there is only one true god that lives in heaven. It teaches that we are all children of that god. It teaches that our heavenly father loves us, but that our life on Earth is a test that he has set for us, and that we can either pass or fail the test. Passing the test means an eternal life with our divine father in heaven. Failing it means being banished from his sight, and eternal punishment in the fire and brimstone of hell.

But are these stories really true? And how, in any event, are we to tell?

Hitchens and others who reject religion rely upon critical thinking. They argue, for example, that if human beings have worshipped thousands of "gods" throughout history—and that if there were only one true god, as Judaism, Christianity, and Islam all assert—then it would follow that most people, if not the vast majority, have actually worshipped the wrong god, or a false god—assuming, of course, that a true god actually exists at all. Most religions teach that we are god's children and that we are physically similar to our gods—despite the fact that they also teach that our gods are immaterial and exist outside of space and time. But what's a contradiction or two among friends? They also teach that our gods, like most parents, want to hear from us—frequently—and that we should, for that reason, pray to them. They teach that our prayers will be heard and answered—if, of course, what we pray for is good in the eyes of our gods—and that we can accordingly help ourselves and others by saying prayers.

These teachings are designed to make us feel very important. Who would not want to be the child of a powerful king—let alone the son or daughter of an omnipotent god? Who would not want to have that god constantly there to watch over us, protect us, and guide us? Religion helps us to create an internal dialogue that confirms what we most want to hear. It tells us that we are important, and why we are important. It helps us forget that we are spinning around one of several quadrillion suns on one of "god knows" how many quadrillion planets in a universe of unfathomable size. It helps us forget that once we are dead, we are truly dead and gone forever. It thus addresses our fear that we are insignificant, abandoned on this earth without guidance. It tells us that we are each very important and, as a species, the center of god's attention.

This is all very nice to hear. But does it not all really strike you as a bit convenient and pretentious? Isn't it more likely that you and I are not the children of god, not the center of the universe, and not the focal point of supernatural attention?

I agree with Hitchens that religion flatters our conceit and selfishness while pretending to teach us modesty. And I also agree that this is the joke of it. Religion pretends to promote humility, while it actually promotes the most outrageous narcissism, vanity, arrogance, and self-centeredness. If you want or need guidance, a father figure, or a direction in life, and if you want or need to always be the center of attention, then you can rest assured that religion will provide it without your having to think too much or too deeply about it. Religion will also teach you respect for authority and conformity. It will, in short, fulfill the needs and desires that parents typically fulfill for their young children. And this, perhaps, is why it all somehow reminds me of a small child calling out to his parents, "Mom, Dad, look at me! Look at me!"

As children we feel special because we are the focus of our parents' love, approval, and attention. We want to be "good" to receive their praise. As adults, we look for that same feeling in various ways. Some of us look for that feeling through organized religion and some of us look for it through spirituality without organized religion. We want to believe the stories that place us in a special position and we want the approval of a super-parent. And woe to anyone who contradicts the stories we tell ourselves. Plato noted that anyone challenging the worldview of his cave dwellers would be vilified. Cicero said, "The wise are instructed by reason; ordinary minds by experience; the stupid, by necessity; and brutes by instinct." Bertrand Russell said, "If a man is offered a fact which goes against his instincts, he will scrutinize it closely, and unless the evidence is overwhelming, he will refuse to believe it. If, on the other hand, he is offered something which affords a reason for acting in accordance to his instincts, he will accept it even on the slightest evidence." Karl Popper wrote, "No rational argument will have a rational effect on a man who does not want to adopt a rational attitude." Anyone who has lived in a religious country knows that they will be ostracized if they question their religion. So if you want or need the authority of a community, then religion is the place to go. But if you want to learn how to think for yourself and make your own judgments, then you will need to look somewhere else.

Plato may have underestimated the capacity of people to absorb new ideas without losing their sense of identity. Many have questioned or rejected religious indoctrination. My own attitude is similar to that of H. G. Wells: "There was a time when I believed in the story and the scheme of salvation, so far as I could understand it, just as I believed there was a Devil"—but "suddenly the light broke through to me and I saw a silly story"—and one that each generation nowadays swallows with greater difficulty. Why do people go on pretending about this? Saul Bellow knew that "[a] great deal of intelligence can be invested in ignorance when the need for illusion is deep." I think people go on pretending because the need for illusion is indeed very deep. But you may, if you read further, decide to cut your chains and turn around to see the world casting its shadows on the cave wall. You might, if you are a movie fan, liken it to taking the red pill offered in *The Matrix* that allows you to see reality in all its beauty and horror.

But before you panic at the prospect of cutting your chains or swallowing the red pill, let me assure you that there are positive effects to casting aside your religious chains. These include greater personal integrity, a greater sense of personal responsibility, greater freedom of thought, less fear of the unknown, and a deeper sense of human morality. Contrary to what you might initially think, living without religion opens the door to your exploring, developing, and consciously adopting moral beliefs and values. The fact that many individuals and cultures have thrived, and continue to thrive, without religion is a clear indication that morality does not spring from religious beliefs. But let me return to these positive and hopeful themes after discussing what typically makes us religious.

In the hilarious 1991 comedy-fantasy film *Defending Your Life*, Albert Brooks and Meryl Streep portray characters who have died and have arrived in a beautiful, dreamlike city where people stand trial to determine whether they should be allowed to move on to the next level of existence or sent back to earth to continue their personal development through successive reincarnated lives. The tribunals are distinctly nonreligious and focus upon one particular issue to determine whether a person is ready to progress to the next level—namely, whether they had sufficiently overcome their fears during their most recent life to move on to a higher plane of existence beyond the grave. The film captures the anxieties that most of us have as young people—of being embarrassed in front of our friends, of not being popular or fitting in, of not being special or sufficiently loved—and the importance of conquering those fears in order to mature into healthy adults. Yes, there are echoes of Siddhartha, but the film simply points out how riddled we are with fear, and how we need to overcome them.

Religion, on the other hand, actually plays upon our fears in its efforts to control us. Instead of encouraging us to conquer our fears, it offers illusions and "deals" as a substitute for confronting and overcoming them. Here, I talk as if religion were something that someone is trying to impose upon us (which it is in the sense that parents and elders do this in many societies), but the fact of the matter is that religion is something that we have created ourselves, and something that in the broader sense we impose upon ourselves. Indeed, the recognition of the fact that human beings create religions in order to assuage our own fears is the first step toward eradicating both the fears that led us to create religion, and the fears that our religious doctrines and practices have subsequently imposed upon us.

The idea that religion is a human creation—that it is man-made and not instituted by a god or supernatural being—can be traced at least back to ancient Greece. But it was not until the eighteenth century that it began to seem possible to finally show what had previously been mere speculation. Ludwig Feuerbach, drawing on Hegel's philosophy, put forth the idea that religions and religious beliefs are a manifestation of the psychological process that Sigmund Freud would later call wish fulfillment. The idea of God, according to Feuerbach, is a human projection that humans make in response to some of their strongest fears and desires. If we are willing to buy into religion, then we can escape from our fears, and live in blissful ignorance of our mortality. This in large part accounts for religion's attraction, and for the strength of its grip on human minds. But for the process to work we cannot consciously decide to adopt a religion as a means to escape from our fears. The decision must be subconscious.

I believe that Feuerbach was right in saying that religions and religious beliefs are human creations, that they are generated by some of the fears that people have, and that the fears that generate them typically correspond to some of the desires that people have. These corresponding fears and desires create powerful emotions that drive people to embrace religion and religious belief. In what follows, I want to explore some of them. My purpose in exploring them is to suggest that we should be hyperskeptical of accepting religions and religious doctrines if only because our personal psychological makeups—by which I mean our individual sets of fears and corresponding desires—virtually compel us to embrace them. These fears and desires are, in a nutshell, the reasons why most people believe in religions and religious doctrines. Bertrand Russell once said, "Fear is the main source of superstition, and one of the main sources of cruelty," and "To conquer fear is the beginning of wisdom." In short, religions and religious beliefs are superstitions, and the hyperskepticism I recommend toward religions and religious beliefs is both the appropriate response to superstition and our best first step on the road toward wisdom.

But what, exactly, are the fears and desires that I am talking about? There probably is no one exhaustive list of them, but table 1 should give you some idea of what I have in mind.

Keep in mind, however, that our fears and desires are not neatly boxed in our minds. They overlap and interact with each other in a myriad of interesting ways. Some of our fears and desires are more dominant than others, and some of them are more dominant in some people than they are in others. Some of us may have some of these fears and desires and not others. And I am sure that some of you can provide other fears and desires that I have neglected to mention. So I do not want to suggest, or be misinterpreted as suggesting, that these fears and desires are in anyway universal to all human beings, or that they are the only ones that might drive us toward religion, or that each of us has each of them to some degree or another. But that said, I think that if you recognize any of them in yourself, then you are well on your way toward understanding what I am talking about. So let's briefly explore each of them in turn.

Table 1. Fears and Desires That Lead to Religious Belief

FEARS	DESIRES
Death	Immortality
The Unknown	Certainty
Powerlessness	Control
Being alone	Guidance and direction
Insecurity	Safety
Rejection	Love
Punishment	Forgiveness
Responsibility	Unaccountability
Meaninglessness	Meaning in life
God	God

Fear of Death

Fear of death is perhaps the single most powerful reason for embracing religion. Indeed, Christopher Hitchens went so far as to say, "Religion will die out when we stop worrying about death." Be this as it may, every religion that I know about teaches that we do not need to fear death, or, more precisely, that death is not real in one way or another, typically because some non-bodily part of us—either "our souls" or "our spirits," but sometimes "our memories" or even the memories that others have of us—will survive the death of our bodies. They teach that some part of us is immortal, that we will survive the death of our bodies, and that we will not be alone after we die. This near-universal promise of life after death underscores just how common the fear of death is. Religions say, in short, that there is not really such a thing as death if, but typically only if, we believe.

Some religions that prohibit sexual license during our lives promise good times with numerous lusty virgins in the next life. (Who would have thought?) Others promise an afterlife in which we are reunited with loved ones who are now presumably all healthy and in the prime of life even though they are dead. This may sound good to some people but I think it is a bedtime story for children. How about telling this bedtime story instead? When we die everything will be as it was before we were born. The Scottish philosopher David Hume told this story hundreds of years ago. It doesn't sound all that bad to me. Hume did not have any children of his own. But I tell it to my kids at bedtime when they express fear of dying and they seem perfectly happy with it.

Desire for Immortality

Our desire for immortality is a counterpart to our fear of death. I feel a deep resistance to the idea that we are dead and gone once we die, and that we are dead and gone forever. Do you feel it too? To avoid this idea, we have children, impart our values to them, and participate in our communities with the hope of leaving the world a better place to live: a better place to paint, or write, or play tennis, or do whatever it is that we might like to do. This is not to say that these activities would not be enjoyable in and of themselves, but I think it is likely they also have at least a subtext of our desire for immortality in them. Most of us want at least some small part of ourselves to survive the death of our bodies. We want to leave some part of ourselves behind.

However, this subtext of our desire for immortality is ultimately insufficient for many, if not, indeed, most, people. We want an eternal afterlife in which we can continue to think and do many if not most of the things that we did during life. So most religions promise it—or, if not that, then eternal rest. This is a basic theme of most religions: we are so special that our essence—our souls—will never, ever, truly perish. Religions thus offer us immortality in exchange for certain actions while on earth—such as believing in a god, supporting a synagogue, church, or mosque, obeying religious elders, and being "good" (as the elders define it) so that a "just" god will reward us after death.

Many people today say that they cannot understand how or why an Islamist terrorist would commit suicide. But how can we not understand an Islamist terrorist's martyrdom when his expectations of immortality so closely mirror the beliefs that most of our "mainstream" religions trumpet? This is not to justify the terrorist's actions, far from it, but rather to point out their consistency with the virtually universal religious teachings that promise the reward of immortality in exchange for religious fealty.

Fear of the Unknown

A close corollary to the fear of death is the fear of the unknown. For death, of course, is the great unknown for all of us. But quite aside from death, most of us feel uncomfortable not having answers to the big questions about life, such as, "How did the universe begin?"

"How did life begin?" "How did we ourselves come to exist?," "Is there any reason or purpose or meaning for our existence?" "And why, in any event, is there something rather than nothing?" We feel that we do not know anything at all about these things and that our lack of knowledge may have very harmful consequences for our lives. We feel that there must be answers to these questions even if we cannot know them and sometimes feel that we cannot live without them. We are all philosophers when it comes to wondering about the unknown and, as philosophers, we could, and perhaps should, all take comfort in the Socratic wisdom that we are wise in knowing how little we know.

But religion instead offers us answers by providing us with simple—though in my view superficial and wholly unsatisfactory— answers to the big questions of life, often insisting that its answers and explanations cannot be understood and must be accepted on faith. The message that there is an all-good, all-knowing, all-powerful, all-just, and all-merciful god who created the universe and everything in it, including us, out of nothing, who loves us and is constantly watching over us, who is there to protect us from Satan and the forces of evil, and who demands only our love and our faith and our obedience in return, is one such answer. Better in my view just to admit that we lack the answers.

Desire for Certainty

Our desire for certainty is the counterpart to our fear of the unknown, and religion, to that extent, accordingly offers us the certainty of faith. Feeling certain does not of course answer whether something is true or not, for the things that we feel certain about may ultimately turn out to be false. But feeling certain that there is a super being who has a mind somewhat like our own, and who knows the answers to all those big questions, can help us deal with our fear of the unknown, even if we do not know the answers to all those big questions ourselves.

Feeling certain that there is an all-powerful god who is responsible for the creation of the universe and its continued existence does not move us one whit closer to a real explanation of anything whatsoever. It may make us feel better to think that we at least have a framework to answer those really big questions in life. But a framework for answers is not actually an answer itself. Indeed, what we are really saying is that there are answers to those questions and that someone else knows them and that this is good enough, even if we ourselves do not know what they are and could never understand them even if we could somehow know them.

What would happen if we simply accepted the fact that there are some things about life that we do not and indeed cannot know, let alone understand—and just left it at that? That might be terrible for a child of god. But would it really be so bad for a human being? We could still feel superior to those "lower" animals that cannot handle abstract thought. It would also mean acknowledging that we are on this planet without an ultimate authority to tell us what to do, determine which of us is right and wrong, and decide our disputes. This, however, would be a step in the right direction—the direction of truth and humility—and it would be an honest recognition that we are, for all intents and purposes, in that very situation already.

Religion is not the only example of a belief system that meets our need to believe that there is order or control when there is not. George Soros persuasively argues in *The New Paradigm for Financial Markets* that the belief in an efficient market that seeks equilibrium is fanciful. He calls flawed ideas that result in positive results fertile fantasies. The common thread between the inability of the establishment to accept Soros's theories (which recognize uncertainty as a dominant force in economics) and the inability of the establishment to accept the falsity of religion is the overwhelming desire to maintain the false premise of certainty, stability, and control due to the fear that the alternative is worse. In other words, the end justifies the means, because truth might upset the apple cart. Religion and standard economics maintain these myths and, ironically, thereby make the fulfillment of the goals of providing certainty, stability, and control less likely in the long run.

Fear of Powerlessness

"Knowledge is power" is one of the great truths of life. So it is not too surprising that our recognition that we do not know the answers to all those big questions, or even to most of the small ones, may make us feel powerless. The feeling that we are powerless can be very frightening. Death and uncertainty are bad enough. But being powerless means that we have little or no control over our lives and what might happen to us while and after we are alive. This, perhaps, is one of the reasons why we typically imagine our gods to be very powerful—if not, indeed, omnipotent—and why we crave a special relationship with this powerful force.

Desire for Control

Our desire for control over our lives is the natural counterpart to our fear of powerlessness. Being powerless means that we have little or no control over our lives. And one way of gaining more control over our lives is by establishing a personal relationship with a god. We need, in other words, to make the one true super being our own personal super being. This will give us an "in" with the god. It might be called networking on a universal scale! Having a personal relationship with our god gives us a real sense of power. We may not know the answers to the big questions but our god does and we have a special relationship with him. We are not merely animals strolling about on a pale blue rock spinning in a vast universe. We have a personal relationship with the one and only true god in the universe. We may, depending upon our religion, be one of his chosen people—or, if we are one of the meek, a relative of his who will inherit the earth! Moreover we can ask him to help us at any time. This means that we ourselves are powerful, that we have influence and control, that we carry clout, as credit card ads used to say.

It is not uncommon to try to humanize and personify our gods to make ourselves feel even more powerful. Giving a name to god—Jupiter, Zeus, Yahweh, Jesus, or Allah—is one way to do so. Now we not only have a super being, but we can also call him by name. But naming is a curious thing, and it may only give us one more thing to fight about. I recently saw a sign at a demonstration that said "Allah is the only God." I couldn't help but wonder how many people have died over "Allah"—not the deity, but over the name itself. But why should a god's name have any significance at all? Most modern religions claim to recognize only one deity. So wouldn't any and every name for a monotheistic god—the one and only true god—actually refer to the same god? Additionally, put yourself in your god's shoes. Why should we think he has any name at all? Or, indeed, that he is a he—or a she—for that matter? So why should we think that that god has to have a name. Why, indeed, should we think that there is any noise at all, or ears around to hear it, in supernatural space? (Real space is of course a vacuum where sound cannot travel.)

But now let's say your deity's name is Qua and I call it Quo. Wouldn't your god, being all knowing, understand that I have mistakenly called it Quo? And why, in any event, would your god, being all good and all just and all merciful to boot, want to give me a hard time about it? Why wouldn't it simply answer, "Here I am!" when I call it Quo, especially since there is no one else up there? And why shouldn't I call it Jerk if it didn't? These are the kinds of questions that keep some people up at night. Are you among them?

Religion offers us the illusion of control. It was born in part from our natural desire to control the elements that affect our lives. And we simply cannot accept the reality that we are not in control of them. So if someone tells us that we can say a prayer or make an offering that will make it rain, save an ailing relative, or give us justice or wealth, the idea of doing nothing seems unacceptable.

Countless superstitions have sprouted up to address this need. Religion is simply one of them.

Fear of Being Alone

Many people have a fear of being alone, especially if being alone means being without direction and guidance in our lives. Religions deal with our fear of being alone and without guidance and direction in much the same way as they deal with our fear of death. They thus promise us that we will never be alone while we are alive and that we will not be alone after we die. For there is, they tell us, an omnipresent god who will always be there to guide us through life and save us from death. This, of course, is just what we all want to hear. And so it is easy for us to believe it. My response to the fear of being alone after death is, once again, the story that David Hume told us centuries ago. We were all just fine before we were born, and we will all be just fine after we die. This, however, is somewhat different from the fear of being alone and without guidance *during* life, which I will discuss below.

Desire for Guidance and Direction

Most of us need and want guidance and direction during our lives. The world is a very big and potentially dangerous place. We, on the other hand, are small and inexperienced. And so it is natural for us to want help. Most of us did, of course, receive some kind of guidance, direction, and help from our parents when we were first born and very young. But the world didn't get any smaller or less dangerous after we grew up. Many of us would like to have parents who will always be there to watch over us and guide us through life. It should thus be no surprise that religions very often portray their gods as our fathers and mothers. Christianity's God the Father, "Our Father, who art in heaven," is probably the best example. He is usually depicted as an old white man with grayish hair and a long beard. Mary, the Mother of God, is another good example. And so, on a more secular note, is Mother Nature.

The god may be a strict and unforgiving parent, like the fire and brimstone god in the Old Testament, or a more lenient and forgiving parent, like the god of love in the New Testament. But the idea is that they are our heavenly parents who are there to keep us company and give us guidance and direction just as our human parents were there to keep us company and give us guidance and direction when we were children. Indeed, fairies, angels, demons, and humans are often depicted in religious artworks as children in relationship to them.

Now some of us devote a large part of our lives to seeking help, direction, and guidance from our heavenly parents. We try to obtain support from them, if only emotional support, by telling them about our lives, our troubles, and our innermost thoughts, hopes, plans, desires, and fears. Religions typically tell us that we can "receive" help, direction, and guidance from them in one of two ways: either directly by praying to our heavenly parents for their help, guidance, and support; or indirectly through other people who say that they know what our heavenly parents think and can pass that precious information along to us—typically at a price. This process also purportedly offers a chance to be heard, that is, hope that our prayers will be answered.

So if you want or need guidance, direction, hope, and rules to live by, you can find plenty of people ready and willing to help. They often come dressed in robes: white or black or red or purple robes—but robes. They will claim to be your heavenly parents' earth-bound agents who have a special relationship with them and are thus privy to special knowledge of their rules, which prescribe, of course, the right way to live. Their interpretations of the heavenly rules, if not the rules themselves, may vary from agent to agent. But if you join a church, and buy a robe, you can make a nice living from it!

Fear of Insecurity

Many of us have a deep fear of insecurity. It's not just fear of financial insecurity that inspires it—though that alone is often bad enough—and it's not just death, the unknown, our lack of power, and the prospect of being alone either. It is a fear that Kierkegaard called "the sickness unto death." It is the fear that our very existence itself is insecure, that that thing that we call "we"—that I call "I" and you call "me"—is very fragile, and that it may, at any given moment, simply cease to exist. This, perhaps, is part of the reason why religions typically promise that some spiritual part of us will survive the death of our physical bodies.

The death of our physical bodies is undoubtedly the most visible confirmation that we have good reason to fear for our very existence. For if we identify ourselves with our bodies, then the answer is very clear. Yes, we may convince ourselves that we do survive the death of our bodies. But we do so as dead corpses. And that, of course, is not quite what we had in mind. But even if we reassure ourselves that we, the real and essential we, our minds, our souls, our spirits, or whatever, are different from our physical bodies—for our physical bodies are, after all, physical bodies that we have—we may still fear the possibility that we, the real and essential we, may cease to exist at any moment. This kind of deep existential insecurity may be the root cause of all anxiety. Thinking about it for too long may lead us to recognize that the real question is not so much "Is there life after death?" as "Is there life after life?"—or, perhaps more accurately, "Do we continue to exist after we cease to exist?"

Desire for Safety

Our fear of insecurity leads quite naturally to our desire for safety. For if we are safe, then we are secure. The two, indeed, might well be regarded as one and the same thing. If the belief that there is an all-powerful and all-knowing god makes us feel safe and secure, then it only underscores the fact that religion can satisfy one of our basic human desires, regardless of whether or not it is true.

But while our desire for safety and security may be perfectly natural, it also has a very real downside to it. For nothing ventured, nothing gained. It may very easily prevent us from taking the kinds of risks we need to experience in order to grow and prosper. You may, for example, be terrified of hell, eternal damnation, burning in lava baths, and whatever other tortures your particular god might have in store for you. You have got to be out of your mind to do anything that risks that kind of punishment. It's much better to be safe, to hedge your bets, to attend religious services, to pay the two dollars to avoid going to hell, even if there's only one chance in a zillion it exists.

Pascal, who thought a little about wagers, argued that believing in God has no downside. If you are right, you are right and have nothing to fear. If you are wrong, you are wrong and still have nothing to fear. But you may, on the other hand, have a problem if you don't believe in God and are wrong. So why take the chance? More to the point, though, in Pascal's France, the only real choice was between atheism and Catholicism. Today, there are countless variants of Christianity, Middle Eastern religious sects, New Age religions, among many others. So the "right" choice may be Vishnu. Pascal's dilemma is of no relevance since the binary decision no longer exists, thereby changing the odds of the wager. So even if you give into your fears, your chances of being "wrong" are now dramatically higher.

What a foundation for civilization! Cowardice is no basis for anything. It takes real courage to refuse to go along with religion just to be safe. But there are real upsides to not going along with religion, including, for example, saving yourself the time, energy, and indignity in worshiping something that does not exist. You also free yourself from worrying about the wrath of a nonexistent entity. You obtain the prize of being free and willing to think for yourself (see chapter 5). But more to the point, Pascal's wager has absolutely nothing to do with whether or not a god actually exists. It only underscores how much we want to be safe.

Fear of Rejection

Yet another fear that drives us toward religion is our fear of rejection. This fear goes hand in hand with our fear of insecurity and our fear of being alone—and with our desire for safety, guidance, and direction. But it is also somewhat different. Being rejected by any person or organization that we want to accept us can lead to sadness and depression. Most of us have experienced it at one level or another. Being rejected, whether by a college, a high school sports team, the "in" group, or a potential girlfriend or boyfriend, is typically a painful coming-of-age experience. Even as adults, we often have an emotional response when being rejected for a job or even a credit card, let alone when being fired from a job, getting divorced, or being shunned by your children. We fear rejection because it hurts.

The psychologists tell us rejection can have detrimental effects upon our emotions, our thinking, our behavior, and even our bodies. They say that these effects may include surges of anger and aggression, which, in turn, may lead us to look for and find fault in ourselves for being rejected, which, in turn, may lead to low self-esteem and self-worth. They say that our fear of rejection had an important evolutionary function, since the rejection of our prehistoric ancestors from their tribes often quite literally meant death. There are ways to treat the wounds that being rejected may inflict. Religion is one of these ways.

Desire for Love

Acceptance is the opposite of rejection, so it may seem as if our desire for acceptance should be the natural counterpart to our fear of rejection. And there is some truth to this. My sense, regardless of the old Groucho Marx joke about never wanting to be a member of any club that would accept him, is that we all want to be accepted by every club that might possibly accept us—if only so that we can decide whether we want to join it. But a desire to be accepted is ultimately a proxy for a desire to be loved. What we want is not merely to be accepted by this or that person, but to be loved as well.

This is particularly true when it comes to religion—and especially when it comes to god. Our desire for acceptance is a desire to be accepted *as we are*, and with all our warts. It is a desire to be accepted by some person or group as *one of them*. But this is not, and cannot be, true when it comes to god. For regardless of whether we were made in the image and likeness of god, we all know that we are not just like god—we wouldn't need a god if we were—and cannot be accepted as just like him. For we are, after all, neither omnipotent nor omniscient. Nor are we the creator of the universe and everything in it.

But religions often condition acceptance by setting behavior that must be complied with prior to acceptance. For example, there is that dirty little business of sin—both the original sin we have supposedly inherited from our original ancestors and the nonoriginal sins we have committed all by ourselves—and our sins will have to be expunged from our souls in one way or another before we can be accepted by them.

Love, on the other hand, is different. Love can be unconditional. True love always is and god's love according to religion is undoubtedly of the true love kind. So religions offer god's love while simultaneously refusing to accept us before we expunge all those warts from our souls. This, of course, is what many people want.

Fear of Punishment

Those who believe in a god generally fear the prospect of divine punishment of one form or another. This, of course, is part and parcel of the idea that our life on Earth is a kind of test to see whether we will worship and obey the god who created us and behave in certain prescribed manners to earn his approval. Passing the test, as we have already said, typically means eternal salvation with god in heaven. Failing it, on the other hand, may mean not only eternal punishment in the flames of hell, but other tortures that may be graphically depicted in paintings on the walls of a church. Our gods, for this reason, are often cast as despots. They may be cast as benevolent despots who can be remarkably kind and generous. But they are nonetheless despots, which means that they can also be very jealous, very demanding, and very punitive—sometimes viciously punitive—toward those "sinners" who fail the test. The punishment that we receive may have the desirable effect of expunging the sins that led to our receiving it. And this is very convenient for religions that need your money and support! But most people do not want to be punished—it may be painful, embarrassing, and very detrimental for our credit reports—and many people thus exhibit a palpable fear at the very mention of the word. Thus, fear of punishment is a powerful emotion compelling people to embrace religion and comply with its behavioral rules.

Desire for Forgiveness

The flip side of our fear of punishment is our desire for forgiveness. Yes, we may have sinned but we are then punished for a "reason." While the punishment was painful and humiliating, it means that our sins were forgiven, and that we may, in effect, start all over again. Being forgiven means that we can once again be admitted into the community of religious believers. It means our acceptance, respect, approval, and validation, both as members of that community of religious believers, and as human beings. Being part of a church, temple, or mosque addresses a related basic human instinct, namely the herd mentality that in ancient times drew people together to enhance prospects of survival. Another way to think of this is that we want to be "good." As children, being "good" meant behaving in a manner consistent with the rules of our parents. This resulted in praise from them, or at least no punishment. As adults, we find in a deity a parental substitute that sets the standard for "good" behavior through religious rules, enables those who comply to perceive themselves as "good," and, importantly, facilitates our being perceived as "good" by others (thereby achieving approval or forgiveness).

In the United States it is possible to be accepted in human society without having a religion to forgive you your sins. But in much of the world, secular society is not very strong, and in some places it may not even exist at all. In these places, you cannot be forgiven your sins and accepted back into the community without stamping some religious party's membership card. In these places religion offers us everything anyone could ask for in terms of forgiveness. We can renew our membership in a respected, exclusive, and sometimes secretive club. And with membership there are privileges. We can speak our own language, eat our own foods, sing our own songs, and wear our own robes. (I really do prefer royal blue.) We can also talk with our own god in our own way. Our very survival and chances for successful mating and reproduction may be tied to membership.

All of this is, I suggest, based upon a delusion, but if it is, then it is a delusion that is shared with all of the other members of "our" religious group. Since we share our delusions with them, we will all have the same honored traditions that bind us together, and we will always be accepted, and respected, by the community so long as we demonstrate belief in its god and obey its rules. This is nothing to sneeze at. Some religious communities trace their roots back thousands of years. If you are born into one of them, virtually all of the people you love and who love you will share a tradition that is automatically yours by accident of birth. They will all care about you and try to educate you properly as determined by their beliefs and traditions. The most vocal members of the group will likely be 100 percent certain that everything that they teach you is

100 percent correct. And if, by chance, they make a mistake, they will be forgiven.

Fear of Responsibility

Our fear of being responsible for our own lives is closely related to our desire for a god to direct and guide us. If there were a god in charge, then we would not be in charge, or at least not fully in charge, of our lives. So, if our lives were not working out as we had hoped, it would not be our fault. We could, on the contrary, blame fate or destiny, and not ourselves, for whatever went wrong. We ourselves would not be responsible. Doing what we were told to do relieves us of responsibility for doing it: "Just following orders, mate!" This works especially well when we are simply obeying some religious agent—priest, rabbi, mullah, etc.—who in turn is purportedly simply passing along the orders that a god has given. If we are only doing the will of god, then, we are absolutely absolved of responsibility. Congratulations! Merely by believing in a divine being, we are relieved of responsibility to exert any effort to build our own lives or to help others.

This aspect of faith is quite dangerous, particularly when leaders believe that they are not fully responsible for their own actions or for the consequences of those actions. When combined with an internal dialogue involving a mission from a deity, the danger is compounded. Moreover, if you also believe that this life is not finite (you will live forever) or that you will return in some other form, this also heightens the sense that what you do now does not matter.

Desire for Unaccountability

The desire for unaccountability is one of the great pulls of religion. We may, no doubt, get divine orders to do things that we do not want to do, just as Abraham got a divine order to sacrifice his only son. But if we believe in a god and know that we must do whatever he/she/it commands us to do, then we are relieved of responsibility for making our own decisions about what we should do, or how we should build our lives, or whether we should help others—provided, of course, that we actually follow through and do what our god wants us to do.

We do not, for example, need to struggle with questions about how we live our lives (according to god's will, of course), or how we should behave in any given situation in which we might find ourselves (just ask ourselves what Jesus would do), or how we should treat the infidels (just check the Quran for that). This aspect of faith is particularly dangerous in leaders who believe that they are on some kind of a divine mission and thus are not fully responsible for their own actions or the consequences of their actions—and especially if they also believe that they will live forever with their god after they die. These beliefs, which are standard fare for true believers, reinforce the idea that we are not responsible, or accountable, for what we do here and now, so long as it is in accordance with our god's will.

Fear of Meaninglessness

If we delve more deeply into our fears and desires, we find a fear of the possibility that our lives are actually and inherently meaninglessness—without purpose, design, and goals of any kind—and a profound desire to identify something that gives meaning to them. In his 1946 book *Man's Search for Meaning*, Viktor E. Frankel, a psychiatrist and survivor of the Holocaust, suggests that our need to find meaning in our lives is even more powerful than our survival instinct. Whether or not this is true is beside the point. It is very clear that we all search for meaning in our lives. We search, in other words, for a purpose, an aim, or a goal in life.

Frankel wrote that meaning can be found through love, achievement, spiritual satisfaction, and suffering. The mix of these elements differs person by person, but the meaning of life that we find—either the meaning of life in general or the meaning of an individual's particular life—is, for many if not most of us, a prerequisite for happiness and quite literally what makes life worth living.

Desire for Meaning in Life

Religion gives us the feeling that our lives are meaningful and important. This is yet another powerful psychological draw to religion. But it also creates an exaggerated sense of self. It can lead us to think that we are somehow on a mission directed from above—that we are fulfilling the wishes of our god. It is inspirational and powerful. It allows us to say things and to do things that we otherwise might not say or do, because we believe our words and actions are justified due to a divine plan or mission. Such a belief can lead to remarkable altruism—to a life of charity and positive deeds—and to unthinkable cruelty—to a life in which killing those who don't believe as we do seems logical and justifiable.

I recently heard a fascinating talk in which the speaker argued that we have the ability to create a sense of happiness regardless of our circumstances. As examples, he noted how one person who had been humiliated in public life and another who had been wrongfully imprisoned for a long period of time both described their presumably negative experiences in glowing terms—as positive life-changing ones. His point was that we find meaning in life by adjusting to adversity, and that we typically do so by creating a story about our experiences to tell ourselves. And the story we choose to tell matters.

Creating a good story about our life is what gives meaning to it. It is one of the keys to our survival. Another is our ability to lie to others and ourselves by creating a meaningful image and role for ourselves in the story we tell. We value artworks, for example, for their history as well as the aesthetic impression they make upon us. Indeed, the aesthetic impression they make very often depends upon their history. Thus, a beautiful painting attributed to a three-year-old "*wunderkind*" loses much of its value once we discover it was actually painted by her mother.

It would be delightful if finding meaning in life were simple, and it certainly can be for religious believers. Following certain rules and living a certain way dictated by religion gives their lives meaning. And if you believe it, it works! Today it seems obvious that many religiously inspired terrorists have followed this logic. But those who would defend us against terrorism by invoking other religious doctrines follow the very same logic, albeit, perhaps, without the violence. In this way, the powerful desire or even need to perceive meaning in life reinforces the attractiveness of a religion for those within its gravitational pull. One may think of it as a planet using all of the fears and desires that we have discussed above to pull in those who are not strong enough to break its force. The question is whether we can create a story as good as the religious story to break free from religion and to give meaning to our lives.

Fear of God

The final fear that motivates us to follow religion is the fear of god him/her/itself. People who believe in a god generally fear that god to one degree or another, just as they may have feared a parent when they were young. They may worry that god will punish them for their sins (as discussed above). Or they may fear in wonder and awe at the power and majesty of the almighty in comparison with themselves. Or they may experience angst or dread—Kierkegaard's "the sickness unto death." As mentioned, religions typically cast their gods as benevolent despots—remarkably kind and generous despots, but despots nonetheless who can be jealous and viciously punitive, particularly toward those who do not worship them. These are very convenient character traits for a god to have if you want followers of your religion to obey whatever you tell them their god wants them to do. They are also convenient character traits for your god to have if your religion happens to need your money and support!

But convenient or not, many people, as I have already said, are downright terrified of god's punishment—of going to hell, of eternal damnation, of burning in lava baths, etc.—and since their god is, when all is said and done, the operative cause of all of these potential punishments, their fear of god's punishment ultimately translates into a fear of their own god. In turn, this fear of their god leads many, if not most, to have an even greater desire for their god, thus creating a self-reinforcing cycle.

Desire for God

One might think that our fear of god might lead people not to a desire for god, but to a desire that god does *not* exist. Our desire for god is really a proxy for all of those other desires that might assuage all our other fears. Our desire for god is really shorthand for our desire for immortality, certainty, control, guidance, direction, safety, love, forgiveness, unaccountability, meaning in life, and so on. It is a way of desiring all of those things at once and in just one word—for it is only an omnipotent, omniscient, super being that could possibly give them to us—and it is, in the end, ultimately the desire that we have to be that omnipotent, omniscient, super being ourselves.

Our desire for god is thus ultimately a desire to be god. For this would be what we would become were we to somehow fulfill all of those desires. But it is also a trap. For regardless of whether we believe that we were created in the image and likeness of god, and regardless of all of the religious authorities that have told us that we were, we are ultimately human beings who must, or at least, should, make our own decisions for ourselves. Believing that we can fulfill all of our desires by believing that there is a god who can fulfill them for us only sets us up for disillusionment and disappointment if and when we realize that our beliefs are false. We will become disillusioned with life as it really is, since life as it really is does not, and cannot, measure up to life as religions tell us it could be. Worse still, religion prevents us from trying to figure out who we are, what we might do, and who we might become if we take our lives and our own decisions into our own hands. In this sense it leads to the antithesis of self-actualization. And it prevents us from being happy with being fallible human beings, since we can never be as good as an infallible god.

3

THE JOURNEY OUT OF THE CAVE

Finding a Path with Critical Thinking

If the Quran or the Bible is all that you have ever known, and if your elders have taught you from day one that "The Book" is "The Truth," then how can you possibly question your beliefs? This is the problem that many of us face. Not only do our fears and desires distort our thinking, but we are also bound by rich quasi-religious, quasi-ethnic cultures whose beliefs and traditions define our lives. These religions and cultures have rules that influence, or in some cases dictate, where we can live, whom we can talk with, what foods we can eat, when we can eat, when we must wake and sleep, how often we must pray, where we must face in praying, whether and where we can go to school, and with whom we may sleep and marry. Imagine trying to find a way out of religion if you were raised as a devout Muslim in Algiers, Istanbul, or Tehran, where the call to prayer echoes throughout the city five times a day, beginning well before sunrise!

These cultural mandates are just a few of the impediments that bar us from a future without religion. For in addition to their rich cultures and traditions, religions also pass along their ancient prejudices and hatreds. And there are very many of them. They may provide us with an identity, yet they typically do so by excluding others. In many societies children are never even exposed to secular thinking, except to be told that those who do not worship as *we* worship are pagans or infidels who, according to at least one "good book," may be enslaved, raped, tortured, or even killed with impunity.

The very idea of leaving one's religio-cultural circle can literally seem suicidal. Even were you not a member, you may naturally seek membership in some circle if only to survive in a world made up of circles. For it can be very lonely out there on your own. Membership in a religion can provide many benefits, including social and financial ones, but there are also downsides to belonging to a religious circle, since, just like other cliques or rings, members of one group tend to fight members of another group. Indeed, some of our best known and most respected religious rings have been fighting each other—enslaving, raping, torturing, and killing each other—for hundreds and thousands of years. This, perhaps more than anything, may be the best reason to find a way out.

But even if you had the temerity to question the foundations of your religion, how would you separate your faith from the culture it springs from and defines who you are? What would you do about the family ties, the cultural traditions, the language, and all the food? These things are separate from the faith itself, but they are all presented to us in an enduring bundle. How would you explain the shadows on Plato's cave wall? Wouldn't you fear being cast out? Who are you to question the elders? These are very difficult problems. But would you have any difficulty today questioning an old legal verdict in light of new evidence? For example, if the great jurist Oliver Wendell Holmes himself had sat on a nineteenth-century jury that convicted a man of murder, would you not question the decision today if modern technology, such as DNA testing, demonstrated the man's innocence? Of course not! Holmes and the others on the jury simply did not have the scientific facts that they needed. New facts alter prior conclusions.

So, is there a way out? Yes. For you as an individual or for your children all you need is determination and effort. But the way out for society must await the cumulative effect of individual decisions to show an impact. We will have to find a nonreligious way to deal with our fears and desires if we no longer want religion to play a role in our lives. The path will be especially hard if you are encapsulated in a religious cocoon, but below I offer some suggestions to help you find your way out. Keep in mind, however, that this book is only in part about giving you a path out. Rather, it is primarily designed with a more modest goal in mind: to encourage you to raise your children without religion.

The key to the way out is critical thinking—including the recognition of our place in the universe and our psychological predisposition to embrace religion. These points undercut the "truth" of religion, challenging the likelihood of its being real and, hopefully, causing you to entertain serious doubts in that regard.

The way out is further facilitated by measuring the good religion does against the bad. That is, in today's world, is religion on balance beneficial to human flourishing or detrimental to it? While this question has nothing to do with whether gods are real, it has much to do with the practical decision about the role you want religion to play in your life, in your children's lives, and in society at large. As I argue, most, if not all, religions have abused their power down through the ages and will no doubt continue to do so in the future unless we as parents take action now.

The Use and Abuse of Religious Power

Fears and desires are not the only forces that lead us to religion. Religious institutions themselves and the centuries-long powerful roles they exert in our societies also play a role in perpetuating religion's hold over us. They are well organized, influential, and well financed. They have a great deal of power that they can use for brand promotion. They generally benefit by perpetuating the religious status quo and by acting as a powerful force in buttressing it. Karl Marx notoriously said that religion is the opium of the people and religion is a big business that is promoted to the masses like an all-healing drug.

Many religions shamelessly exploit their brand and abuse their power for material gain. Indeed, the whole history of religion is one of amassing and holding power and property. The Catholic Church in its heyday and contemporary Islamic fundamentalist sects are just two examples. But it's not just the wealth and power that they have already amassed; its also their ongoing ability to attract capital that perpetuates their enterprise. Religious institutions employ people who can make a very good living by persuading other people to give them money—or by taking it from them—and by obtaining special tax-exempt status and other special economic and social treatment from governments. These people may enjoy the feeling of being respected by others or exercising power over others. While there are some who may genuinely believe and practice what they preach, we must nonetheless note the psychological and material benefits that can be derived from a ministry if we want to assess whether a specific religious leader is motivated by power or greed.

But it's not just financial power and profit. For the people who hold and exercise religious power periodically abuse it for their own sexual gratification. The Catholic Church and Islam provide the most recent example of such abuse. Catholic priests have notoriously used their position to prey on young boys and ISIS terrorists claim that the Quran gives them the right to rape non-Muslim women.

Then there is also the political abuse. In many parts of the world, including the Middle East, religious institutions *are* the government, and there are a great number of people spending time and money to maintain its power. Religious bureaucracy, like government bureaucracy, is self-perpetuating, and it jealously guards its income streams. There may be competing brands, but they all share the basic formula. Just like competitors who cooperate in trade unions, they have no problem singing the same tune—"More tax exemptions for religion"—to promote their interests while maintaining that their individual brand is the best. But all of this could, perhaps, be forgivable were it not for all of the violence and bloodshed.

Mark Twain famously wrote:

> Man is the religious animal. He is the only religious animal. He is the only animal that has the True Religion, several of them. He is the only animal that loves his neighbor as himself and cuts his throat, if his theology isn't straight. He has made a graveyard of the globe in trying his honest best to smooth his brother's path to happiness and heaven.

The power of religious leaders is difficult to challenge because they claim that their authority is divinely derived from god. It should not come as a great surprise that our political and business leaders also continue to promote religion and religious beliefs, as doing so is a time-proven technique for bolstering their power bases and income streams both because of the appeal to believers and the implication that a deity supports their leadership.

By putting it this way, I am simply echoing Thomas Paine, who wrote, "All natural institutions of churches, whether Jewish, Christian, or Turkish, appear to me no other than human inventions, set up to terrify and enslave mankind, and monopolize power and profit."

Religious doctrines and institutions have always been a primary cause of violence. This is because they inevitably perpetuate their prejudices against and hatreds of other religious sects, and their members, by claiming, explicitly or implicitly, that their brand is the "one true" brand and that using other brands condemns people to eternal damnation. The idea that other brands are just as good is anathema to the survival of each religious institution. Indeed, when Pope Francis had the temerity to suggest that atheists who live good lives can also go to heaven, the Vatican, quick as you can say "undercuts our market," immediately issued a statement backtracking on the idea. This makes perfect sense. For if atheists and non-Catholics can go to heaven, then why bother to be a Catholic at all? If you can get all those virgins without becoming a martyr, then why bother to blow yourself up or murder other people?

Because religions are big businesses that compete with each other for customers, it is unrealistic to expect any religious institution to welcome the members of another faith into its fold or to encourage them to break down the barriers that separate them. They all benefit from their brand identifications and maintaining them is just one of the ways in which religions use and abuse their power.

The persecution of Galileo is a good example of religion's use and abuse of power. Galileo was born in 1564, arriving just days after Michelangelo's death. He was a contemporary of Johannes Kepler, who encouraged him to publicly support Copernicus, a Polish monk who had argued that the sun might well be the center of our solar system. Galileo eventually published a book in 1632—translated into English in 1661 as *The Systeme of the World: in Four Dialogues* (also translated as *Dialogue Concerning the Two Chief World Systems*)—arguing that the Earth goes around the Sun, instead of the Sun going around the Earth. The threat that Copernicus, Galileo, and this book posed to the Catholic Church soon became obvious. For if the Earth orbits the Sun, then it cannot be the center of the solar system, as the Church had taught. And if the Earth is not the center of the solar system, then man cannot be located in the center of the universe, with all that this implies—

none of which was very good for the religious teachings of the Catholic Church. For religious myths depend on an appropriate sense of scale. So moving mankind from the center of the universe to one of several planets that orbit the Sun was not especially helpful for maintaining the myth! Why would God send his son to Earth if it is not of celestial importance? The Church accordingly threatened to torture or kill Galileo if he did not stop saying that the Earth goes around the Sun. Thus threatened, Galileo stopped saying it.

Galileo regarded the Church's threat as very real. He knew that its Inquisition had already burnt Giordano Bruno at the stake for teaching ideas that were not so different from his own. So he eventually recanted his ideas, writing, "I do not hold the Copernican opinion, and have not held it after being ordered by injunction to abandon it." This, of course, left some ambiguity to the matter, and his subsequent trial left unsettled whether Copernican concepts were heretical or Galileo had been convicted of breach of contract, that is, for promoting Copernican ideas after agreeing not to do so. Galileo lived under house arrest thereafter. But the problems that he raised for the Church became all the more severe as scientists learned just how insignificant our physical location in the universe really is. In this, Galileo was also instrumental.

Galileo may not have been the first to use a telescope or to point it at the moon, but he appears to have been the first to understand the significance of what he saw. The shadows of mountains and craters that he observed on the Moon meant that it is a terrestrial body like the Earth, and not the perfectly smooth crystalline celestial body it had previously been thought to be. He also figured out that the "stars" orbiting Jupiter are actually moons that reflect sunlight, just as our Moon does, and that this constitutes another proof of the Copernican system. He further undercut the Church's story by showing that the Earth itself is not stable and that, even though we cannot feel it, we are standing on a spinning globe that is orbiting the Sun.

All of this only scratches the surface of Galileo's threat to the Church. Galileo had the temerity to say that arguments require proof, that people should think for themselves instead of accepting ideas on faith, and that simply showing that some earlier authority held some view is not enough to establish the truth of that view (an argument still resisted even today.) Thus, in his masterpiece *The Systeme of the World: in Four Dialogues*, Galileo has his character Simplicio speak for the Church, Aristotle, and the established world order—and his character Salviati speak for the learned world, Copernicus, and himself. In the Second Dialogue, he famously has Salviati urge Simplicio "to come with arguments or demonstrations of your own, or of Aristotle, and bring us no more Texts and naked authorities, for our disputes are about the Sensible World, and not one of Paper." The point, of course, is that merely citing some text—such as the Bible—is insufficient to support a substantive position. Previous "authorities" may be mistaken so we must give reasons that those whom we wish to persuade can understand, question, and criticize if we hope to convince people that what we are saying is true.

There are plenty of books that chronicle the violence committed in the name of religion through the ages and continuing through to the present. As Christopher Hitchens noted, you cannot name a good act that could have been inspired only by religion, but you can point to countless horrific acts inspired by religion that could not have been committed by a nonbeliever.

From a cost-benefit perspective, religion fares poorly. Let's turn our attention to how to escape the cycle of violence related to religion by exploring ways out.

A Way Out of the Cave

In a nutshell, the way out is, as mentioned, through critical thinking. For me, the first step was to understand our psychological predispositions toward religion. I find it useful to carefully follow the reasoning of a profound thinker in this arena to buttress the points I made about our psychological predisposition to embrace religion.

Sigmund Freud, the founder of psychoanalysis, wrote, "religion is comparable to a childhood neurosis." He called it "an attempt to get control over the sensory world, in which we are placed, by means of the wish-world." He said that we have developed a wish-world inside our minds due to certain "biological and psychological necessities." He wrote, "If one attempts to assign to religion its place in man's evolution, it seems not so much to be a lasting acquisition, as a parallel to the neurosis which the civilized individual must pass through on his way from childhood to maturity." He said:

> The whole thing is so patently infantile, so foreign to reality, that to anyone with a friendly attitude to humanity it is painful to think that the great majority of mortals will never be able to rise above this view of life. It is still more humiliating to discover how a large number of people living today, who cannot but see that this religion is not tenable, nevertheless try to defend it piece by piece in a series of pitiful rearguard actions.

Freud maintained that "religion is an illusion and it derives its strength from the fact that it falls in with our instinctual desires." He viewed it as infantile and man-made partly because of its obvious link to the desire for a life-long father figure, but also because of its convenient promise of immortality.

But Freud also thought:

> Our own death is indeed quite unimaginable, and whenever we make the attempt to imagine it we ... really survive as spectators. ... At bottom nobody believes in his own death, or to put the same thing in a different way, in the unconscious every one of us is convinced of his own immortality.

And he wrote:

> Our knowledge of the historical worth of certain religious doctrines increases our respect for them, but does not invalidate our proposal that they should cease to be put forward as the reasons for the precepts of civilization. On the contrary! Those historical residues have helped us to view religious teachings, as it were, as neurotic relics, and we may now argue that the time has probably come, as it does in an analytic treatment, for replacing the effects of repression by the results of the rational operation of the intellect.

Freud believed that religion is an expression of underlying psychological neuroses and distress. At various points in his writings, he suggests that belief in religion is an attempt to control the Oedipal complex, a means to give structure to social groups, a wish fulfillment, an infantile delusion, and an attempt to control the outside world. Freud's psychological explanation of religion builds on the ideas of Ludwig Feuerbach, as alluded to above. Feuerbach put forth the idea that God is a projection of the human mind—and Freud added a psychological foundation for it. They both believed that religion is wish fulfillment. But Freud adds the explanation that our adoption of religious beliefs is a reversion to childish patterns of thought in response to our feelings of helplessness and guilt. He thought that we feel a need for security and forgiveness, and so invent god as a source of security and forgiveness. He saw religion as a childish delusion and atheism as a grown-up realism and said that "a religion, even if it calls itself a religion of love, must be hard and unloving to those who do not belong to it."

At times, religious people do make an attempt, or perhaps a pretense, of offering rational verification of wishful thinking in the form of "proofs" of the existence of their gods. Freud recognized this, and spent some time examining them. Unsurprisingly, the defenses against skepticism that he regarded as most common at his time remain very common even today: my religion must be true because it is so very old; my religion must be true because of the success of various proofs; and my religion must be true because it is holy, and any attempt to question it is sinful. But none of these "proofs" impressed Freud any more than they impress critical thinkers today.

Freud was particularly disdainful of attempts to defend religion on the basis of its irrationality. The medieval form of this "proof" was called *Credo quia absurdam* (I believe because it is absurd). The more modern form is the "as if" argument. It is the idea that a belief is true if you live your life "as if" it were true and are thereby made happy. The first "proof" is meaningless at best, as Freud pointed out. For if one absurdity, why not another? If you value absurdity, you cannot rationally choose or prefer any given absurdity over any other. But a similar argument can be raised against the second "proof," since it is not really an argument but an evasion from the obligation to rationally defend one's assertions.

Many people think that accepting a belief on faith is fine in the absence of knowledge. But Freud regarded belief based on the absence of knowledge as a lame excuse, and he was particularly dismayed by our attempts to defend religious beliefs on the grounds that we are justified in believing that something is true so long as it cannot be absolutely proven to be false. He thus argued:

> Ignorance is ignorance; no right to believe anything can be derived from it. In other matters no sensible person will behave so irresponsibly or rest content with such feeble grounds for his opinions and for the line he takes. It is only in the highest and most sacred things that he allows himself to do so.

Another common claim made on behalf of religion is that it is a positive force in human affairs. Today we hear the clarion call from religious leaders for more religion in people's lives in an effort to cure all manner of social ills. Indeed, we often hear that most of these ills would not even exist if it were not for the gradual decline of religion's influence in society over the past few decades.

As discussed above, the cost-benefit analysis does not favor religion. Freud also finds such arguments not credible. Freud believed that both religion and civilization make important contributions in taming the wild instincts of humanity. But he did not believe that religion is a particularly strong force for either order or morality. On the contrary, Freud did not find any evidence that religious believers were any happier or more moral than their non, or less, religious peers. He wrote: "It is doubtful whether men were in general happier at a time when religious doctrines held unrestricted sway; more moral they were certainly not" and "In every age immorality has found no less support in religion than morality has." The implication for Freud was only too clear. If religion has had thousands of years to show what it can do, and if it has not managed to achieve much improvement in human beings, then reason and science should be given a chance.

Freud regarded science and religion as mortal enemies, and he never made an effort to hide this view. On the contrary, he loudly proclaimed it both far and wide. Religion, according to Freud, had proven itself to be a failure, and science must now be given a chance. The heart of his argument thus runs contrary to the aims of those who would try to build bridges between science and religion. For Freud believed that the fundamental premises of science and religion are wholly and irreparably incompatible.

Freud was overly optimistic about science, which is itself a human institution and hence susceptible to all human weaknesses, yet he was very realistic about religion. There are, however, non-Freudian psychologists and psychiatrists and, indeed, whole branches of psychology and psychiatry that have tried to make their peace with religion. (I cannot help but wonder whether this is due to the recognition that taking on religion can ultimately be dangerous to one's income stream.) For example, mainstream social psychology and related fields deal with, as social psychologist

Michael Argyle describes, "biological topics, such as the origins of facial expressions, and some aspects of linguistics," and with most aspects of the psychology of religion. Arguably more rigorous than psychoanalysis, social psychology overlaps with sociology, which assumes, as Argyle continues, that "religion was the result of deprivation and would probably fade away through secularization." But it "avoids taking any position on whether beliefs are true or not." Its "non-ontological approach makes it possible to study these things while making no judgment on their reality." According to Argyle, similarly some psychologists hold the view that "the role of psychology now is to help understand rather than to undermine" religion.

I think that there are many ways out of Plato's cave, but I have devoted so much space to Freud's theories about religion because they are consistent with the thinking that led me away from religion. But regardless of what Freud thought, and regardless of what I think, we appear, as a society, to be driven to embrace religion by the numerous fears and desires that I have discussed above. These fears and desires explain why religion still has such a hold over us even though science has steadily encroached upon its territory with each passing year. For we all have a fear of death, of the unknown, and of our own impotence—and we all feel alone, rejected, and insecure. We all want love, acceptance, and security—and we all create in our minds a sense of reality and our place in it.

These fears and desires lead us to religion. For most of us would really like to believe in magical powers, in the supernatural, and, of course, in omnipotent and omniscient supernatural parents who love us unconditionally and are always ready and willing to defend us. The Force is with us! But how different, in this regard, was an ancient cave man's mental construct of a Fire God from our own mental construct of a Judaic or Christian or Islamic concept of God? So far as I can see, nothing has come down to us through the ages so unchanged from Neanderthal times as our idea of god (with the possible exception of British cooking). Does our psychological predilection for religious belief combined with the facts about our geographic position in the known universe and lack of any scientific evidence supporting the existence of a supernatural being mean that those beliefs are false? My common sense leads me to answer yes. What is your answer?

A second step that may help you think your way out of religion is to embrace science. As Richard Dawkins argues, studying science is one of many ways to escape the strong gravitational pull of religion. I touched on the role of science in debunking religion by beginning my discussion with scientific evidence about our place in the universe, as best we know it today, and then referencing Darwin's contribution. Thus, if you have questions about the big issues (how life began, etc.), an alternative to accepting a god as a substitute for real answers is to pursue the answers yourself by studying or at least accepting that there are no real answers available to some questions yet.

You would find, for example, that science established long ago that molecular building blocks can be created by lightning and common gases that existed on Earth millions of years ago and that exist throughout the universe now. Though science has yet to fully solve the exact origins of life, scientists will eventually discover more about the process by which forms of life began and will adjust earlier findings and models. If you have the energy, brainpower, and discipline, you can study science or read philosophy to develop a secular framework for considering possible answers to the big questions that trouble you.

Many people reject the idea that life could arise and take root without a god out of hand, evidence to the contrary notwithstanding, just as the Church fathers refused to look through Galileo's telescope. But if you reject all of this science without ever studying it, then on what grounds can you possibly be rejecting it?

It is remarkable that the very same people who turn to god because they are unwilling to accept the lack of answers are not troubled in the least by their inability to comprehend "God" or to explain where God came from, or how God was created, or how God can be eternal—or even what eternity actually means. I find it remarkable—given the standard description of God as all knowing, all powerful, and having a reach that spans the billions upon billions of light years of the universe—that anyone can feel comfortable about accepting God's existence without a scintilla of scientific evidence. We are, after all, talking about a supernatural being on a scale totally foreign to human experience and of a level of complexity far greater than that of all known life on earth. This may be what Michel de Montaigne meant when he said that "ignorance is the softest pillow on which a man can rest his head."

So science can help you see the inconsistencies in religions and recognize that religions in fact provide no answers of any sort. Religion merely calls that set of unknown answers God. In this respect, science can help you reason your way out of religion.

As we begin to think about how we might pass our values on to our children without religion, I only ask that you consider the possibility (in my view overwhelming likelihood) that the most basic tenets of religion are false. I hope that these words from Benjamin Franklin's final address to the Constitutional Convention will help you to do so:

> I CONFESS that I do not entirely approve of this Constitution at present; but, sir, I am not sure I shall never approve it, for, having lived long, I have experienced many instances of being obliged, by better information or fuller consideration, to change opinions even on important subjects, which I once thought right, but found to be otherwise. It is therefore that, the older I grow, the more apt I am to doubt my own judgment of others. Most men, indeed, as well as most sects in religion, think themselves in possession of all truth, and that wherever others differ from them, it is so far error. Steele, a Protestant, in a dedication, tells the Pope that the only difference between our two churches in their opinions of the certainty of their doctrine is, the Romish

Church is infallible, and the Church of England is never in the wrong. But, though many private persons think almost as highly of their own infallibility as of that of their sect, few express it so naturally as a certain French lady, who, in a little dispute with her sister, said: "But I meet with nobody but myself that is always in the right." . . .

On the whole, sir, I cannot help expressing a wish that every member of the convention who may still have objections to it, would, with me, on this occasion, doubt a little of his own infallibility.

4

THE NATURE OF MORALITY

Being Good Without God

Let's begin exploring morality and ethics just where you would expect—with a conversation I had over calamari a la plancha with my good friend Gennady, a former KGB colonel, at his favorite restaurant on the main promenade of Puerto Banus in Marbella, Spain. It was during the final months of Gennady's fifty-five years of life. Gennady sported his customary four-day stubble, which gave him a gruff appearance that belied a sparkling upbeat personality and boyish sense of humor. Sensing that he was fading, Gennady had traveled to Amsterdam to enjoy all that it had to offer prior to our dinner in Spain. During that meal, we discussed his businesses, his ex-wife, his children.

During the Soviet era, the KGB was the Ivy League of Russia. It attracted the best and brightest minds in the Soviet Union, and it rewarded them with excellent training in foreign languages, opportunities for travel abroad, access to forbidden literature, and national leadership positions. There were few opportunities outside of government service to attract the Soviet Union's young talent. For this reason, many KGB agents became intellectuals after active service or, in Gennady's case, a real estate developer.

"Rich," Gennady always called me "Rich," both in English and in Russian, "which is more important to you: personal loyalty or principle?" He then offered me his own opinion that principle matters more than loyalty: that you must act in accordance with your ethics even if it goes against the interests of a friend. I was delighted to hear such a deontological defense of duty from my KGB friend!

But regardless of whether you are a former KGB colonel or a noncommissioned parent, you will probably have to consider where moral principles actually come from someday. At this point in my argument, you may be wondering, what, if anything, would take the place of religion if it were no longer honored in our society and passed along from parent to child? Exactly how would children become moral without it? I struggle to look past the irony of this question, given the world's history of religious violence and abuse. But I will do so nonetheless, since parents and philosophically minded friends constantly pose this question to me when I propose that they try to raise their children without religion, along with the question about how society could be structured without it.

The short answer to the first question is that basic morality is natural to human beings, as natural as eating and breathing and growing, and that it is nurtured and passed along through parenting. Watch the Discovery Channel to see how values manifest themselves naturally throughout the animal kingdom! You will see alligators coddling their young in their mouths and apes grieving the deaths of their young. Moral principles are natural, but we can codify them into laws that can be religious, secular, or a mixture of the two. History suggests that the codification of our moral principles eventually became imbued with religious themes (think the Ten Commandments) and over time became purely religious laws in some places, a mixture of religious and secular laws in others, and purely secular laws in still others.

Writing is a relatively new skill set on our planet, being a mere 5,000 years old. (Note: not the planet, the writing skill, lest a young-Earth creationist think I'm conceding one of their unsupportable contentions!) Accordingly, it is hard to be sure what people were saying to each other about morality before writing first appeared. But I think it is likely that many parents were scolding their kids for hitting their siblings, just as we do today. It is also impossible to know whether they colored their parenting lessons with religious overtones a hundred thousand years ago—that is, whether they said, "Don't hit your sister," "Don't hit your sister or you will not be allowed to draw on the cave wall," or "Don't hit your sister or you will be struck down by the lightning god."

But though some of you may believe that morality derives exclusively from religion, there is every reason to explore the concept of societies having morality without it. Christopher Hitchens has persuasively refuted the idea that morality sprang from religion and would disappear without it. I will not repeat his many responses here except to note that to believe that morality sprang from religion is to contend that mankind did not even try to avoid murder, incest, cannibalism, and the like prior to some specific religious revelation.

I must admit that I do not spend any time specifically teaching my kids values. Somehow this happens naturally by their seeing how I behave or how those in their lives behave. Normal conversations about real-life situations also provide opportunities to teach values naturally. But I nonetheless felt vindicated in my view that morality is a natural trait that is often exhibited by mammals as they raise their young when I read an article about the work of Dr. Frans de Waal. De Waal, who studied oxytocin in mammals, noted that the fact that female mammals naturally take care of their young is due to the higher levels of this hormone in females than in males.

Mothers are hardwired to care for their young, and this oxytocin-driven empathy is the essence of our morality, even in dealing with others. In *The Bonobo and the Atheist: In Search of Humanism among the Primates*, De Waal synthesizes empirical evidence that human fairness has natural roots in biology, and explores what that means for the role of religion in human societies.

In an interview with CNN about the book, De Waal addressed some of the concerns about the relationship between morality and religious myths. He noted that northern Europe is in the midst of an experiment to determine whether a moral society can exist without religion. In his view, the experiment is showing that it certainly can. In his own country, the Netherlands, for example, 60 percent of people are nonbelievers. He further noted that he thinks morality is older than religion:

> I find it very hard to believe that 100,000 or 200,000 years ago, our ancestors did not believe in right and wrong, and did not punish bad behavior, did not care about fairness. Very long ago our ancestors had moral systems. Our current institutions are only a couple of thousand years old, which is really not old in the eyes of a biologist. So I think religion came after morality. Religion may have become a codification of morality, and it may fortify it, but it's not the origin of it.

He added that not every helpful action by an animal, including humans, is motivated by some innate or immediate sense of individual selfishness.

> Sometimes people say that everything that humans do or that animals do needs to have a payoff, but that's not true. The example of adoption of children, I basically think it's a costly act with no payoff, and these things happen in animals also. Animals sometimes help each other even between species. Dolphins may help human swimmers, and I don't think the dolphins get much out of it. So individual acts don't necessarily need to have a payoff.

So they are not selfishly motivated. They are really altruistic, but you have the tendency to help, and to have empathy for others in general, on the average, is beneficial. Because you live in a group, you depend on these others, so you need to care about these others also because your survival depends on group life, and so there is some sort of general payoff, but people often think in terms of each individual act needs to (reap) some benefit but that's not necessarily true.

The origins of this sense of empathy among mammals, he argued, are tied to the evolutionary need for effective parenting.

We think that the origin of empathy, in the mammals at least, has to do with maternal care. So a female, whether you're a mouse or an elephant, you need to pay attention to your offspring, you need to react to their emotions when they're cold, or in danger, or hungry, and that's where we think the sensitivity to others' emotions come from.

That also explains why empathy is more developed in females than males, which is true in many animals, and it's true for humans, and it explains the role of oxytocin. Oxytocin is a maternal hormone. If you spray oxytocin into the nostrils of men and women, you get more empathic (empathetic) reactions from them, and so the general thinking about empathy is that it started in the mammals with maternal care, and then from there it spread to other relationships. So men can definitely have empathy, but they on average have a little bit less of it than women.

I agree with De Waal's idea. Biology provides some of the basic primate psychology that humans have, such as our pro-social tendencies, our sense of right and wrong, our sense of fairness, and our predisposition to follow rules. But it does not provide the specific rules that we adopt. I want to emphasize this, because when I say that morality derives from biology, people sometimes think that I mean that every rule we follow can be traced to our biology. I don't think it works that way at all. I think that we have inherited our tendency to follow rules from our primate ancestors, but that we have developed moral rules that are suitable to our specific ways of living.

We are, for example, currently conducting a number of moral debates in the United States—about the rules that pertain, or should pertain, to abortion, gay marriage, immigration, and the like—and years from now we may believe very different things from what we believe today. This means that we should not look for our specific moral rules in biology. But instead of looking at our predisposition to morality itself—our pro-social tendencies, our sense of right and wrong, our sense of fairness, and our disposition to follow rules—as something that we design in our heads, I think we should consider it to be as natural as the survival instinct.

But if our predisposition to morality itself springs from biology, in the form of hormones, as Dr. De Waal argues, then it has nothing to do with religion. Religion may, no doubt, have influenced the specific moral rules that some of us follow. But we would have been predisposed to following certain moral rules with or without it. Religions, however, have falsely claimed to be the wellspring of morality to enhance their brand and bolster their own standing down through the ages. In this sense, they have been free riders on morality.

The Codification of Morality

Although our predisposition to morality does not derive from religion, our specific moral rules have been codified in religious texts just as they have been codified in secular texts. The Code of Hammurabi dating back to about 1772 BCE is an early example of such codification—and the conflation of religion and morality is one of its primary results. Over time people began to think that religious texts such as the Bible and Quran were actually the sources of morality rather than the writings of people codifying morality. This is what I meant in saying that religion free rides on morality: religions claim that they are the source of morality rather than mere reflections of it.

The most obvious example of the nonreligious codification of morality is secular law. It provides guidance in a legal context on all types of moral issues, ranging from social relations among people to property contracts of all kinds. In some places, it consists only of precedent, or the body of decisions that judges have made in similar cases over time. This is called "common law" or "*stare decisis*," and law in the United States is ostensibly of this kind. But secular law is actually codified in some places and much of our law in the United States is codified as well. "Thou shalt not kill" is expressed in very great detail and covers numerous situations in secular law, ranging from intentional killing to negligent acts that cause death.

Secular law addresses basic moral issues in both criminal and civil contexts. If you examine the United States Code or Germany's codified laws, you will learn how people in those countries are supposed to interact with one another in contractual relations, real property matters, civil disputes, and virtually any other real-life human activity you can imagine. Secular codified law does this without reference to any god, and in far greater detail and depth than anything you can find in religious rule books. But fear not, while secular law encompasses a vastly broader array of moral situations and rules than religions seek to address, it covers all of the rules articulated in the Ten Commandments as well.

The Importance of the Rule of Law

Much of the world lives in countries in which the moral values and rules that form the moral foundation of their societies have been derived from their religious elders and laws. But there are, as Dr. De Waal has noted, several countries whose societies are fully functional on a moral level without any religious belief at all on the part of the majority. In much of northern Europe, children are raised with moral values and rules that have nothing to do with edicts put forth by a religion or a mystical entity. Numerous examples of such societies already exist. So it is certainly possible to enjoy life, treat others well, and take responsibility for your own life and your decisions without a religious construct.

Our secular law embodies many of the moral values and rules that have traditionally been ascribed to religion, and many more as well. It provides a legal foundation for our society to protect the weak, defend property, and safeguard freedom, while simultaneously drawing a line to show where, when, and how your freedom may adversely affect mine. Countries that codify their secular law, and that emphasize the rule of law, already have a solid foundation in place for building a moral society that can function without religion. All that is needed are specific laws, a police force, and a judicial system to enforce them. But here, the rule of law, or the idea that we are a nation of laws and not of men, is key. In "traditional" societies in which religious belief is dominant and the rule of law is weak (and this describes many societies of the Middle East), the first step away from the dark ages of religion will be education about the rule of law—as well as parents who are ready and willing to let their children learn about morality, and the other things they will need to succeed in life, without a god and religion.

5

LIFE UNDER THE SUN

Embracing the Benefits of Abandoning Religion

We have now looked at what drives us toward belief in gods, why that belief should be strongly doubted, how to break the cycle, and where our morality and values might come from if they do not come from religion. I personally have no choice but to reject the idea that they come from religion for all the reasons that I have outlined. I simply do not have the mental "off" button that I would need to disengage from critical thinking and allow myself to experience the alleged euphoria of a religious belief and faith that I regard as delusional. You, on the other hand, may still have a choice, and may thus want to hear something more about the personal and societal benefits of *not* having delusional religious beliefs.

So what is the upside of abandoning religion and deciding not to pass our religious beliefs on to our children? What is our internal narrative if we are on our own in the universe—if we are truly without a god to guide us—and have only ourselves and whatever life forms may exist on distant planets to keep us company? What do we get by way of a personal and social gratification—what is our reward—if we take the red pill, or cut ourselves free from chains in Plato's cave? What, in short, is our prize? What gifts are you giving your children?

If what I have been saying is true, then your prize for rejecting what you have been taught about religion includes freedom from fear, freedom to think for yourself, and the joy that comes from embracing uncertainty and acknowledging that you do not in fact know the answers to some important questions. Your prize is that you get to raise your children without any pressure to instill the terror and psychological abuse of fire, brimstone, and an eternity in hell in their gentle little minds. Your prize is that you get to live your life as you wish to live it with no one telling you what to think and what to do in the name of some god, and without any god—Qua, Quo, Santa Claus, or Easter Bunny—always watching, judging, rewarding, or punishing you. Your prize is that you get to think critically and make judgments for yourself instead of parroting religious beliefs and religious doctrines promulgated by religious authorities. Your prize is also the great relief of not having to pay homage to some religion you do not really believe! Think of all the extra time you will have to enjoy freedom!

Richard Dawkins, renowned scientist and author on atheism, shared his thoughts about one aspect of the prize:

> The feeling of awed wonder that science can give us is one of the highest experiences of which the human psyche is capable. It is a deep aesthetic passion to rank with the finest that music and poetry can deliver. It is truly one of the things that make life worth living and it does so, if anything, more effectively if it convinces us that the time we have for living is quite finite. . . . After sleeping through a hundred million centuries we have finally opened our eyes on a sumptuous planet, sparkling with

colour, bountiful with life. Within decades we must close our eyes again. Isn't it a noble, an enlightened way of spending our brief time in the sun, to work at understanding the universe and how we have come to wake up in it? This is how I answer when I am asked—as I am surprisingly often—why I bother to get up in the mornings. To put it the other way round, isn't it sad to go to your grave without ever wondering why you were born? Who, with such a thought, would not spring from bed, eager to resume discovering the world and rejoicing to be a part of it.

Even if you cannot completely extricate yourself from religious indoctrination to fully enjoy the prize, you can free your children. Consider more closely the many gifts such a decision offers.

Greater Freedom to Think Critically

Most religions rely upon religious texts to create the impression that their doctrines are valid and have great authority. They are written down in books after all—often very old ones by unknown authors, giving them an air of mystery! But the validity and authority of a doctrine has nothing to do with whether or when it was written. People point to texts to avoid having to prove the matters contained in them. In the case of religion, the very existence of written texts is supposed to be evidence that a god actually exists. But to simply cite a text, any text, as an authority to prove a point about anything other than that text itself exists is the antithesis of critical thinking. This was Galileo's whole point when he told Simplicio to come with arguments and demonstrations, instead of texts and authorities, since their disagreements were about the real world and not about paper. There is a well-known variation on Simplicio's argument that I like to call the BGSS fallacy. "BGSS," of course, stands for "Because God Said So!" Religious thinkers often appeal to it in one way or another. But I think that this fallacy represents the very height of circular reasoning. This is especially apparent when the faithful point to God's words to prove the existence of God.

It is not easy to explain the value of the prize. But I think Bertrand Russell came close when he wrote:

> Science tells us what we can know, but what we can know is little, and if we forget how much we cannot know we become insensitive to many things of great importance. Theology, on the other hand, induces a dogmatic belief that we have knowledge where in fact we have ignorance, and by so doing generates a kind of impertinent insolence towards the universe. Uncertainty, in the presence of vivid hopes and fears, is painful, but must be endured if we wish to live without the support of comforting fairy tales. It is not good either to forget the questions that philosophy asks, or to persuade ourselves that we have found indubitable answers to them. To teach how to live without certainty, and yet without being paralyzed by hesitation, is perhaps the chief thing that philosophy, in our age, can still do for those who study it.

A Greater Sense of Integrity

Integrity is also part of the prize. Religion is fundamentally at odds with integrity because it often requires deception, irrational thought, and the dissemination of falsehoods in order to obtain and protect the material benefits of being part of the established religious social and political order. I recently spoke with a colleague who heads a huge public company based in a southern U.S. state. We spoke about the subjects in this book and he fully agreed with me. He also views religion as utter nonsense. But he told me that he had no choice but to attend church regularly and pretend to be religious if he wanted to keep his corporate position because he lives and works in a religious milieu that is intolerant of atheists and freethinkers.

If you do not believe in god but pretend to or call yourself "spiritual" to blur the issue, then you too may well be ducking for cover in a society that is hostile to antireligious sentiment. You secretly agree that religion is silly but lack the courage to say so publicly. You don't want to accept the consequences. You want to secure the benefits of membership without truly being a member. You may even have legitimate fears about your physical and financial well-being should you be forthcoming about your actual beliefs. Still, even under such circumstances, which are unfortunately all too common, your personal integrity will likely suffer as a result, for you are essentially living a lie.

Or perhaps your case is somewhat different. Perhaps you see yourself as having "true" faith—a personal religion separate and apart from institutional religion—and do not see yourself as holding that faith for personal gain. Your integrity, however, may still suffer. For how does your faith comport with what science has taught you? Faith had a lot more wiggle room before science started filling in facts where only questions existed before. Can your sense of personal integrity survive if you willfully close your eyes to scientific facts that conflict with your faith? Surely it will suffer if you cannot reconcile the conflict or choose to not even try.

Think about the corrosive effect on society when people who secretly think that religion is nonsense are force-fed a religious diet on a daily basis? This too is an integrity issue. Some say that religion is the foundation of our values and societal rules. So what effect does it have on the credibility of those values and societal rules if we actually believe it is false? Don't we undermine our own moral and societal structure by failing to insist that it be based upon something more solid than ancient myths? Won't we undermine the credibility and legitimacy of our leadership by permitting religion to play a political role? Haven't we, in fact, done so already?

If we do not really believe in religion, then it is only natural that we will perceive those who foist it upon us as lacking credibility, integrity, and sanity. H. L. Mencken once observed "whenever 'A' attempts by law to impose his moral standards upon 'B,' 'A' is most likely a scoundrel." This applies first and foremost to our political leaders. Being "good" must mean more than simply parroting the party line. But if, over time, we can develop the courage to say what many of us really think about religion—namely, that it has been one of the greatest sources of violence and bloodshed that the world has ever known, that we can be good people without it, and that those who practice it should not be respected simply because they practice it but perhaps in spite of it—then the effect may gradually snowball and we might eventually reach a point where we can do without it. This would be a great step forward in the development of an open and civilized society.

It can start with each parent choosing not to pass along an ancient set of lies to their children. By doing so, you get to spare your kids a good deal of the confusing nonsense that you likely had to overcome in your own life. If you are Catholic, you get to give them a life without a sense of guilt from someone else's original sin! And you get to feel proud and altruistic on a broader scale for advancing civilization by removing yourself from the army of unthinking religious warriors who have been clawing at each other's throats for countless centuries.

A Greater Sense of Morality

It may surprise you that you may actually experience a greater sense of morality without the pressure that religion imposes upon people. This recalls Immanuel Kant's tenet that "morality predicated on external pressures alone is never sufficient." He meant that morality should come freely from ourselves, and that we weren't really moral if it didn't. According to Richard Dawkins,

> Over the centuries, we've moved on from Scripture to accumulate precepts of ethical, legal and moral philosophy. We've evolved a liberal consensus of what we regard as underpinnings of decent society, such as the idea that we don't approve of slavery or discrimination on the grounds of race or sex, that we respect free speech and the rights of the individual. All of these things that have become second nature to our morals today owe very

little to religion, and mostly have been won in opposition to the teeth of religion.

Socrates raised the same issue when he asked how a man would behave if he could twist a ring, become invisible, and get away with whatever he liked. Would he behave in the same way he behaves when he thinks that people are looking, or that god is looking? How would you behave? Socrates concluded that being good is its own reward, and that we should not be good simply because other people are watching or because god is watching or because we will get some reward other than being good itself. If you still think that religion is the source of morality, take a close look and compare the conduct of those you regard as religious and those you do not. In my experience, those who proclaim themselves to be religious often do so, either consciously or unconsciously, to justify their hostility toward others, acting, as lawyers might say, under color of authority, which in this case is the authority of their god.

There are countless examples of people who have used religion to justify their hostility toward other people. Adam Hochschild's book *King Leopold's Ghost* illustrates the point. It shows the ties between using a religious cover to mask the horrors of colonialism as Europeans spread the word of God while actually stealing the property of millions of people worldwide and causing their deaths. In the Kingdom of the Congo, the Belgians—yes, the Belgians— killed millions of people at the beginning of the twentieth century by forcing the natives to harvest raw materials, such as ivory and rubber, from the jungle and transport them to distant ports. (The infamous Mr. Kurtz of Joseph's Conrad's *Heart of Darkness* was likely modeled upon a Belgian administrator in the Congo during this time frame named Leon Rom, who placed heads on stakes outside his station.) Religion provided a false moral framework to cover these outrageous acts, and the colonizers used the cloak of faith as a way to frame themselves as worthy of respect and just. In this sense, being a member of a religion is not unlike carrying a party card in communist societies. Indeed, I think that often there is an inverse relationship between being religious and being moral if one looks at the history of religious violence, abuse, and appropriation.

We can all too easily assume that since we are religious we are by definition "good." This simple formulation relieves us of the need to analyze whether we are behaving morally/ethically. The fact is that we do not need to pass a moral test to belong to a religious organization—just being born is typically enough to do the trick. But if you were not born into a religion, you can usually walk through the door, pay a few dollars, and, ipso facto, you will be blessed (become a member) and, now being blessed, you are moral too. Simple and silly.

Life is filled with numerous, complex moral and ethical issues—and introducing religion only clouds the questions surrounding them.

I have personally found myself on the wrong side of ethical issues on several occasions. When, for example, my law firm decided to represent the tobacco industry in a few cases, I did not resign and stayed on for quite a while because I quite frankly needed the money. I spoke up against taking these cases, and I undoubtedly cost myself money by doing so. My view was that a major legal firm like ours should not be complicit in defending a business that kills a million Americans annually and countless other millions worldwide. I argued that we should not help grow their business or go to court to keep them from being regulated or restricted. I agreed that everyone is entitled to legal counsel in a criminal context, but I argued that these cases were not about criminal law and, more importantly, that the tobacco industry was not entitled to the best legal minds or to the legitimacy conferred by association with a law firm of sterling reputation. "Let them get other lawyers!" I in essence suggested, about as successfully as Marie Antoinette when she said, "Let them eat cake!"

I did not think it was enough to say that we were getting paid well and that our client's activities were legal. For I think that the immorality of actions is heightened by the wealth of the actor. A person who takes the same questionable actions because he is poor and trying to support his family should be judged by a different standard than one who takes such questionable actions despite the fact that he is well off. This sliding scale affected my ethical judgment, and ultimately my view of these cases, but I did not immediately leave the firm when it added tobacco clients to the thousands of other corporations it represented.

In my view, that something is legal, such as the sale of tobacco, does not mean that it is moral. Morality is an individual decision not a collective one. Consider, for example, the Dred Scott decision in 1857 in which the Supreme Court of the United States effectively endorsed slavery. That made slavery legal until the case was reversed long afterward—but it did not, of course, make it moral.

On another occassion, I found myself in the fascinating position of being the only American advising a firm that represented the inner circle of the Russian government, first under Boris Yeltsin and later under Vladimir Putin. During the Yeltsin years, I had a very satisfying experience in Moscow leading legal reform in Russia. But once Putin rose to power, my personal views were no longer welcome and I felt that I would be complicit in building and maintaining a dictatorship if I continued to try to help his government. This was not exactly what I wanted to do, and I exited, stage left, as soon as I felt I safely could.

I did not leave before learning quite a bit about the mindset of oligarchs. It is founded upon a mentality of entitlement not unlike the entitlement highly religious people exhibit in justifying their indifference to those with less wealth. The oligarchs do not base their attitude on being the chosen ones as religious conservatives often do—that some are better off than others due to God's will—but rather on a medieval moral framework along the lines of might makes right.

A Greater Chance to Live Your Own Life

Life without religion can be, and should be, both peaceful and satisfying. You can live happily and morally without it. You do not need to pledge your allegiance to a religion or to a church, mosque, or temple in order to maintain close bonds to your family members, neighbors, friends, and other loved ones in your life. Nor, I think, do you need to blur the distinction between reality and fantasy, or to give yourself over to delusional thinking, or to belief in supernatural beings and supernatural explanations. But you may still desire a little "magic" to bring up your kids, so at the outset of the next chapter, I offer a few ideas about how you can help yourself and your children enjoy their lives with a touch of "magic" without blurring fantasy and reality.

* * *

I am often asked whether my view amounts to atheism or agnosticism. I think that it is impossible to prove to a certainty virtually anything, including that god doesn't exist or that religion is false. So you would not be mistaken if you called my view agnosticism.

There is, however, an important caveat. In our everyday lives, we are all accustomed to making judgments about what is real and what is not. That stars exist is something we generally accept as fact, because we see the sun and seem to feel its warmth. That we really see stars in a distant galaxy by their images being projected on a giant TV screen in our solar system is possible too. But I would like to see some evidence before regarding it as a serious possibility. Anyone who proposes a theory that runs counter to massive evidence bears the burden of proof to establish the truth of that theory. As Richard Dawkins stated in a 1996 lecture titled "Science, Delusion and the Appetite for Wonder,"

It really comes down to parsimony, economy of explanation. It is possible that your car engine is driven by psychokinetic energy, but if it looks like a petrol engine, smells like a petrol engine and performs exactly as well as a petrol engine, the sensible working hypothesis is that it is a petrol engine. Telepathy and possession by the spirits of the dead are not ruled out as a matter of principle. There is certainly nothing impossible about abduction by aliens in UFOs. One day it may be happen. But on grounds of probability it should be kept as an explanation of last resort. It is unparsimonious, demanding more than routinely weak evidence before we should believe it. If you hear hooves clip-clopping down a London street, it could be a zebra or even a unicorn, but, before we assume that it's anything other than a horse, we should demand a certain minimal standard of evidence.

By the same standard, I personally view the existence of a supernatural entity with a conscious mind that controls the universe to be a theoretical possibility—but one that I regard as belonging to the category of utter nonsense requiring powerful evidence before becoming worthy of discussion. I thus think that agnosticism would be a misleading description of my view as it gives far too much dignity to what I regard as nonsensical ideas. Nontheism would probably be a more accurate characterization.

But anyone who wants to live a life without religion must be ready to address nihilism—which in this context is the idea that life would be meaningless and not worth living if there were no god. My own view, however, is very different: we are very lucky to have this short window of life and can do wonderful things for others and ourselves if we so chose. While I have acquaintances that are remarkably self-centered, I also have friends who seem to conceive of life as a competition to see who can do the most good during their years on the planet. So just living and finding meaning in life may, ironically, be enough to satisfy your need for meaning of life! For most of us, survival and helping others survive provides meaning in life. Working to feed, house, and clothe ourselves and our loved ones can be a very meaningful task—as can our efforts to improve our material situations, solve our intellectual or professional challenges, and enhance our statures within our social and business communities. Raising our children well and enjoying their company is a profoundly meaningful experience for most of us that dwarfs virtually all other experiences, but there are many other activities that can provide meaning and joy to life, including education, the arts, sports, and relationships, to name a very few.

6

THE EARTHBOUND PARENT

Raising Good Children Without Religion

Children crave "magic" and we, as parents, eagerly try to provide it to them with our stories about Santa Claus, the Easter Bunny, the Tooth Fairy, Father Frost, and countless other imaginary forces. We love watching them react with joy in their eyes as they listen to us recite tales that excite their imaginations. There is nothing wrong with encouraging make-believe fantasies in young children, and rejecting religion is fully consistent with doing so. Some parents end that magical period for their children and try to prepare them for the real world of adulthood by gently revealing that there is no Santa Claus, no Easter Bunny, and no Tooth Fairy. Others allow their kids to figure it out for themselves, and still others do nothing whatsoever to destroy their children's belief in fantasy and fairy dust and magic. They substitute religion instead.

Is it a good idea to introduce our kids to the "magic" of religion even if we know or suspect it is false? I suggest not. Do we pass along religion so our kids can share in our own fantasies without even considering alternatives? How can we help our children to formulate a more satisfying life enhancing inner dialogue than the one religion provides? The key to answering these questions is to think for yourself and do what you think is best for them. We all have the ability and the responsibility to use our powers of critical thinking to benefit our children. My own position is that you can do this best by ending the fantasy and magic at whatever age you think is appropriate for your child.

If you have ventured this far, you may now be considering raising your children without religion and wondering how to do it. Persuading you to raise your child to be a critical thinker and making suggestions regarding how to do it are two different things. The former is the "why-to" portion of this book and the latter the "how-to" element that we now turn to in this chapter.

Let me begin by acknowledging that there are myriad ways to raise children and that you as the parent are the one who gets to decide which path to choose. This "how-to" discussion is meant only to provide some ideas and examples for your consideration, not to set out a formulaic prescription for parenting. My suggestions are intended to assist you in making choices that will benefit your child and your family. After providing some general principles that illuminate my own parenting philosophy, I will focus upon parenting elements that pertain specifically to raising secular children.

General Parenting Tips

I have tried to instill in my children an intellectual curiosity and a fervent desire to figure things out for themselves—to rely on their own powers of critical thinking instead of religious texts. I have helped raise four of them successfully (admittedly, by my own measure) and I am well aware of the stresses and challenges of parenting a child for the stresses and challenges of the real world.

It is very difficult to make a living, maintain close relationships, stay rested and healthy, and maybe attend night school while simultaneously finding the time and energy to be a great parent. But my guess is that you, like me, really want to do it. So I would like to give you a few practical parenting tips that I have found useful in raising my own children. They emphasize encouragement, humor, positive modeling, active parenting, and education.

Create a Parenting Plan

Reach an agreement with your spouse regarding the key elements you want to emphasize in raising your children—and review it periodically. Parents rarely agree on everything regarding how to raise a child and indeed in my experience the deep love parents have for children causes them to fight over the smallest details in how a child is raised. For example, in my culture babies should be kept away from drafts and bitter cold but in my wife's culture, fresh air on a daily basis is a must. Thus, I endured the torture of watching her place my precious babies in a carriage outdoors in the freezing Moscow winters to enjoy the fresh air! (Don't worry, though, she bundled them up and they survived.) As you struggle to agree on the main principles with your spouse, keep in mind that differences are to be expected and that your strong feelings attest to your love for your child. Compromise even if it means setting up a family structure that is somewhat different than what you experienced as a child. While it is difficult to alter the mental hard wiring that resulted from your early years, just remember that your spouse's hard wiring is not the same as yours so compromise is a necessity.

You might begin by finding areas of likely common ground. These could include exploring your respective aspirations for your child in various aspects of life. Do you both want your child to be well educated, to enjoy learning, to try various sports and activities? Which ones? Do you want your child to be ethical (a "good" person) and to treat others well? Do you have role models in mind for your child such as grandparents, friends, or public figures past and present? What are your views on the tone of interaction with your child and the type of relationship you want to establish as parents? Can you agree on how to discipline children at various stages of their development?

If you periodically try to coordinate with your spouse in parental planning, you will have a much better shot at achieving your goals than if you remain silent and just go your separate ways in parenting.

Spend Time with Your Kids

The single best thing that you can do to insure your children's emotional well-being and set a foundation for their future is to spend time with them. While telling them that you love them is a fabulous thing to do, even better is to show them that you do by being with them. You can do this by witnessing their lives. This means paying attention to them when they want to show you something or share an achievement such as drawing a picture in school. You can talk, play, walk, read, and interact with them from day one through their entire lifetimes. It is the rare day that I do not play tag with my little girls or pretend to be the tickle monster—then again, maybe I am not pretending—run!

You can shoot baskets with them, kick soccer balls, play piano together, have them sit on your knee reading or solving chess puzzles, listen to stories, accompany them on play dates, and teach them to tie their shoes. If you do not do these and a thousand other fun things with your kids, you are in my opinion, not only depriving them of wonderful parenting but you yourself are also missing the very best parts of your life.

Set the Culture and Activities in Your Family

It is your job to decide how your kids spend their time in their early years. While I consider what other people do with their children's time, my wife and I put this to one side when we make this important decision, because it affects who my children will become. If, for example, you choose to have the family gather around the kitchen table for dinner each night, it will happen. If instead, you want each person to grab a bite on his own, that family culture will evolve. Do you want to spend an hour on Thursday nights enjoying a family talent show where the kids sing and dance? Go for it. You set the patterns and activities.

Most people in the United States spend large amounts of time on passive entertainment such as TV, video games, social networking, and various apps. Much of this fits in the category of living vicariously, meaning watching others engage in fun activities and taking pleasure through their experiences. Indeed, the passive vicarious "activity" of watching TV has become accepted as a social event, where families or friends gather to spend time watching TV together. People also do this to feel part of our culture and to fill time in the day. The average American watches TV more than five hours a day. While there is certainly a place for passive entertainment and a place for the social bonding that occurs while watching TV together or discussing a popular TV show at the water cooler with colleagues, as a parent you may want to consider whether you really want to pass along the habit of that passive approach to life to your children. Do you want it to be a central feature of their existence and a primary focus of their social interactivity?

As discussed in more detail below, there is no TV in my home, and I would suggest that you get rid of your television too, though I understand how difficult it is to even consider such heresy! My wife and I allow our kids to watch some shows and movies online, but only with our approval. That the vast majority of families plop their kids in front of the television is no reason for you to do the same. It is simply not in the best interests of your children in my opinion.

Take Responsibility for Educating Your Children

If you cut out TV, you will have a big void to fill or, more accurately, a huge amount of time for your kids to acquire life skills and to learn! For example, as parents who value being citizens of the world, my wife and I are raising our children to be multilingual. How do we do this? I communicate with them in English but my wife, who is Russian, speaks and sings to them only in Russian. In addition, we are fortunate enough to be able to afford an au pair who does the same in Mandarin. As a result, they are fluent in English, Russian, and Mandarin, and I will encourage them to learn a Romance language or two as they grow older.

Importantly, learning a new language should not feel like work for a young child. It is best acquired through interactions with caretakers or peers but can be supplemented in other ways, such as through songs, games, and, yes, even TV programs. When my wife and I do allow our children to watch shows online, we typically have them watch programs either in Russian or Mandarin. This has led to some amusing surprises. At one point my youngest daughter heard Mickey Mouse in a cartoon and said to my wife in shock, "Mickey is speaking English." She had apparently been watching Mickey only in Russian cartoons up to that point!

I certainly realize that the choices my wife and I have made in this regard may not be feasible for all parents, whether for economic or other reasons. Indeed, you may be a couple or even single parent with very limited support and financial means. But if you have access to the Internet, you can use that to expose your child to things other than TV shows, such as music and languages. If you have family members or friends watching your kids, consider what knowledge they can impart. If you plan to send your child to a preschool or afterschool program, consider one that offers immersion in a foreign language. It is up to you to decide what approach best aligns with your values and means. If all of this sounds daunting, keep in mind that in many regions of the world children are raised to speak two or more languages, such as in many parts of Africa, Asia, and Europe. There is no reason your child cannot speak a second language too if you come up with a plan to regularly expose her to it.

Take Responsibility for Yourself

To be the parent that you wish to become requires more than anything else courage, by which I mean the courage to use your own mind to make decisions (don't just go along with what others do) and then to put them into action yourself (don't wait for others to do it for you.) Here are some practical suggestions that may help you be the best role model and parent you can be:

- Chart your own course. Trust your own judgment and make your own decisions. Listen to advice from others, but run from those who want to instruct as the spokesperson of a supernatural authority.

- Find balance in life. Unless you have an overwhelming passion for just one thing, make room for yourself, your family and friends, sports, education, and hobbies that keep you growing and learning.

- Have fun doing great things now. Do something courageous and positive during the time you have on the planet. Don't waste your time praying to something that does not exist as if this will help make something happen or listening to advice from people who claim to know what that something that does not exist may be thinking. (As Carl Sagan said, "Life is but a momentary glimpse of the wonder of the astonishing universe, and it is sad to see so many dreaming it away on spiritual fantasy.")

- Use all of your muscles, including your brain, to strengthen them and make them last. Thinking is great fun.

- Work on overcoming your fears. Don't fear the truth about who you really are. Live positively, looking for the good in yourself and in others.

- Treat others politely and respectfully, but remember that this does not necessarily imply showing respect for their opinions or beliefs. You are free to disagree with opinions and beliefs.

- Take responsibility for yourself—including your education, your health, your behavior, in short, for all of your life—no matter what your circumstances. Do not expect things from supernatural beings or impersonal authorities like a government.

- Be genuinely humble. You are unique but certainly not divine. Find meaning in life through your accomplishments, goals, love, devotion, and sacrifices. One step each day can make a difference in your life and in the lives of others. (Noted Bertrand Russell, "The main things which seem to me important on their own account, and not merely as means to other things, are knowledge, art, instinctive happiness, and relations of friendship or affection.")

- When you're feeling low, keep your game face on with your children. (Troops have morale problems, not officers.) Stay connected with people and think about helping others.

- Hold your kids and tell them that you love them out loud and with your eyes.

Secular Parenting Tips

Turning now from general parenting ideas to specific ways to raise children without religion, I offer the following six suggestions. (For specific answers to common questions about secular parenting, see the appendix.)

Reduce Exposure to Religion

My first suggestion is obvious: if you wish to raise your children without religion, do not introduce them to religion when they are young. This means not exposing them to religious gatherings, religious songs, religious books, and religious entertainment.

"Easier said than done" may be your response. You may feel that you live in a religious environment where religion is omnipresent (much like the deity religions vaguely describe). Actually, though, I would hazard a guess that you already dramatically limit exposure to religion without being fully aware of your actions. Please allow me to explain. Devil worshippers and other marginal theological sect practitioners gather and worship throughout the world, yet your young children are blissfully unaware of this. Why, because you do not expose them to it.

You may respond that such low-profile religious groups are easy to avoid. Fair enough, but if you are Catholic you likely do not take your children to Jewish temples or Islamic mosques. My point is that if you practice a religion, you are likely involved in but one religion and you exclude from your life, and the lives of your children, all the other supernatural belief systems in the world to the extent feasible. Thus, you already do what I am suggesting to a large extent. (You also do this in other contexts. For example, you probably limit your child's exposure to cigarette smoking by avoiding movies showing smoking or avoiding situations where people are smoking in real life. You probably limit their exposure to sex, violence, and alcohol up to a certain age as well.)

If you are religious, taking the step of avoiding exposure to all religions amounts to purging from your activity diet the one religion you have not eliminated already, namely the one you were exposed to by your parents, unless you are one of the rare people who switched to a different religion during your life. If you want to raise secular children, do not take your children to a church, temple, or mosque, do not sing them songs about religious figures, and do not read stories to them with religious themes or watch movies that bring to life religious stories. If you must interact with religious institutions or traditions for food, clothing, childcare, or other necessities, explain to your child at an appropriate age the distinction between the culture of a religion (such as its ethical instruction) and its acceptance of the supernatural as real.

What happens on a practical everyday level if you never expose your children to these influences (or cease doing so if you have already started)? Ending participation in ceremonies and exposure to religious-flavored entertainment has a tremendously positive ripple effect throughout your family life.

Your thoughts will not be occupied by questions about what a deity supposedly did, what powers the deity has, or how the deity can hurt or help you

Your conversations at home will not revolve around or be informed by the rules of religious doctrine, the edicts of religious leaders, or the demands of worship. There will be no prayers before meals but perhaps a thank you to whoever prepared the food or bought it. The conversations will be about your lives, activities, people you know, places you've been or wish to go to, things you've learned or experienced, problems to solve, and chores to do, and the songs you hum as you fold laundry will be secular tunes not religious hymns.

Your vocabulary will change in small ways too. For example, if you wish someone well and want to show you care about them, you might say, "Have a good day," "Be careful out there," "All the best", "Love ya," "Live Long and Prosper," or "I wish you well," instead of "God bless you," "Godspeed," or "Vaya con Dios."

Your friends will be drawn from a broader swath of society, because your exposure to people will be less restricted and encompass places other than buildings in which like-minded people congregate to worship a supernatural being.

If you are already enmeshed in a religious lifestyle, then there may be some small level of effort required on your part to provide substitutes for the religiously oriented stories and songs that are being eliminated. For example, if you decide to stop reading religious stories to your children, you may need to get some new books for the shelf. Fortunately, the market is overflowing with books that are devoid of religion, and they are easily found on Amazon or Google by typing in "Children's Books." (Not so hard!) Almost everything that pops up is secular. If you cannot afford to purchase books, try your local library. If you lack access to a library, try borrowing books or accessing stories on the Internet. Moreover, if you live in a country in which the public schools are not affiliated with a religion, you'll find a treasure trove of secular material in them designed to promote critical thinking in children.

The same applies to movies and entertainment. In the United States, most entertainment is secular, so it is easy to avoid religious material if you just pay a little attention to what you show your children starting from a very early age. Whether they watch Disney, Cartoon Network, Nickelodeon, PBS, or countless other sources of children's entertainment, there is plenty to see that does not expose them to supernatural belief systems. (This is not to suggest that I advocate a large diet of entertainment!)

What about music? Easy peasy as my six-year-old would say. Just enter as your search term on the Internet "Children's Music" or "Children's Nursery Rhymes" and a whole world opens up to you. Add your own language to the search if you are getting songs in the wrong language, though you probably already have Internet and keyboarding in the language you wish.

The Internet and most public libraries in the United States contain a wonderfully rich selection of books and visual entertainment suitable for various ages chock full of ethically nutritional content for the palate of every parent. It is up to you to choose what you want your child to experience. You have countless alternatives to a religious diet for your child's eyes, ears, and mind.

Moreover, by the time you read these words, the alternatives available to you will have expanded, so be sure to explore the latest technologies delivering content to your home so you can choose what you want for your child. All you have to do is spend a few minutes just once to find some places on the Internet you like, and you will have an easy starting point as your child grows to supply plenty of nonreligious content.

What takes the place of conversations relating to religion? Having raised my two sets of children without religion, I can attest that imaginary deities and their minions never entered the stream of conversation with or consciousness of (as best I can determine) my children. The early years with children, as most parents will find, are spent playing with them, cleaning up after them, feeding them, driving or escorting them, chasing after them, and talking to them or to others in front of them. Had we been discussing religious gatherings, no doubt in time my children would have learned words associated with such rituals and observed our attitude toward religion. But since we are not religious, other subjects have occupied our conversations spanning the full spectrum of family life. Depending on their age and our lifestyle at the time, the kids have heard us discuss shopping, errands, school, homework, music, scheduling, housekeeping, work, problems, other people, business, politics, money, the world, and the respective failures of each spouse to live up to the other's expectations (fights).

But this does not mean that our children lacked imagination or exposure to magic. To the contrary, we encouraged this during their childhoods through countless secular imaginary characters (think Disney) while not shying away from periodically integrating various characters that are loosely associated with religions such as Santa Claus, Father Frost, the Easter Bunny, witches, and the like. As to the latter group, we included these quasi-religious fantasy figures because it was impractical to avoid all exposure to these characters in our society and we saw no real downside in this limited exposure since the kids perceived the characters in a nonreligious context. Having these characters in common with their friends and participating in periodic rituals also gave the kids a sense of social connectivity.

The result has been great fun!! We have a Christmas tree each year and give some gifts on that day. We also have a large celebration at New Years and treat that as our main holiday gift-giving time.

You might well ask why I encouraged fantasy-involving nonreligious characters but discouraged fantasy with religious connotations such as devils or gods. As mentioned, children crave fantasy, it is part of being imaginative and this should in my view be cherished with regard to nonreligious characters. The bond created with other children who enjoy the same characters is also very valuable to your child.

My reasons for shielding the kids from religious characters incorporates all of the reasons discussed above regarding the benefits of being grounded in reality rather than fantasy. Moreover, in my society, religion is not identified as fantasy, so I would run the risk of fostering confusion in my children when they found that some people treat devils, for example, as real creatures while we the parents do not. While they will eventually learn that their parents see religion in a very different light than most people in the world do, I want them to be old enough to understand the issues when this difference becomes evident to them.

The starkness of the difference between our views and the views of many others is well illustrated in an interview with the late Supreme Court Justice Antonin Scalia, who had the confidence and poise to articulate his perspectives with great clarity in a conversation with *New York Magazine*.

Interviewer: You believe in heaven and hell?

Scalia: Oh, of course I do. Don't you believe in heaven and hell?

Interviewer: No.

Scalia: Oh, my.

Interviewer: Does that mean I'm not going?

Scalia: [*Laughing.*] Unfortunately not!

Interviewer: Wait, to heaven or hell?

Scalia: It doesn't mean you're not going to hell, just because you don't believe in it. That's Catholic doctrine! Everyone is going one place or the other.

Interviewer: But you don't have to be a Catholic to get into heaven? Or believe in it?

Scalia: Of course not!

Interviewer: Oh. So you don't know where I'm going. Thank God.

Scalia: I don't know where you're going. I don't even know whether Judas Iscariot is in hell. I mean, that's what the pope meant when he said, "Who am I to judge?" He may have recanted and had severe penance just before he died. Who knows?

Interviewer: Can we talk about your drafting process—

Scalia: [*Leans in, stage-whispers.*] I even believe in the Devil.

Interviewer: You do?

Scalia: Of course! Yeah, he's a real person. Hey, c'mon, that's standard Catholic doctrine! Every Catholic believes that.

When my kids came across devils and gods in books and movies, they viewed them as they would any fantasy figure they might find in a Disney film, though over time they came to realize that some people believe these characters are real.

If I lived on a deserted island, I could safely read stories to my children about a bearded old man who created and controlled our island, the sea, and the universe beyond us confident that if I presented this as just a fun story, my child would accept it as such. Even if I pretended this were real, the children would figure out that this is a fun fantasy just around the time they figured out that I am Santa Claus. But you and I do not live on an isolated island, so we must as parents take into account societal factors that may affect our children, including the possibility that a child will hear the old bearded man story from adults who believe it to be factual. Conversely, I am perfectly happy to see my kids enjoy the Easter Bunny traditions because I have no concern that society will confuse them by presenting this tale (pun intended) as real.

Kids need fantasy! Your challenge is to be certain that you know the difference between reality and fantasy so you can impart that knowledge to your child.

In sum, by eliminating exposure to religion, you alter the subjects you discuss with your child. What you end up talking about with your child in the absence of religion depends almost entirely upon the menu of activities you establish. This subject, as it happens, is our next topic!

Create an Active Secular Life for Your Child

If you are highly religious, you may be able to disassociate yourself at least in part from the responsibility of raising your child by a belief that fate or providence (divine guidance) overrides your input. A deity's plan or other supernatural controlling forces trumps your own. If, however, you conclude that we are alone in the sense of having no supernatural supervision, then you as a parent are entirely responsible for the life you created and, in the early years, for how you fill that life. I can think of no greater joy or responsibility than raising a child, so enjoy this period of your life.

Whether you do so thoughtfully and consciously or haphazardly and indifferently, you as a parent will be the major influence over your child's life. By your mere interaction with your child you teach: language, movements, facial expressions, facts, concepts, athletics, emotions, behavior, values, and philosophy, among many other things. You also largely select the third parties that will influence your children, such as friends and teachers, by virtue of your decisions about the community you choose to live in.

Some parents have no idea that they are teaching a child just by interacting with them or by establishing a network of influences through choice of a school or community. The best parents, though, and you are likely among them since you care enough to read this book, give thought to how they wish to raise their child and take steps to responsibly execute a plan. This applies equally to wealthy or poor parents since planning can take into account financial capabilities.

Let's explore plans that go beyond the basics of teaching your children to eat well, drink water, sleep enough, exercise often, be social, avoid drugs, and become educated. You will doubtless convey those thoughts and help your children fill their time each day with activities relating to these basic functions. How do you want to fill the rest of their day at any given age? What are you trying to achieve as a parent? I would encourage you to be courageous in dreaming for your child in the sense of pursuing a parenting path and taking active steps to implement it. You may make mistakes but you will do more for your child this way than a parent who merely prays for results!

Let's consider a variety of plans that you may wish to consider. Whether you are a tiger mom who wants her child to excel in a particular activity, a father who dreams of a well-balanced child with broad interests, or a parent who wants to raise a laid-back "smell the roses" hedonist, you likely want to give your child a chance to be happy, which often translates into providing a good start in life as measured by the vision you have in mind for your child.

Please do not overlook the marketing angle as you select a plan and activities for your children that correlate to your vision. Children want to feel good about themselves, so be sure to help them feel proud about what they are doing and learning under your supervision. It is my view that, as they get older, virtually everything they do is in some manner calculated to make themselves more sexually attractive, whether by dress, movements, activities, etc. (Don't worry. This will not last forever. It ends somewhere around age ninety.) In subtle ways help your children understand that the way you are raising them makes them special and attractive both in their early years and as they age to dovetail with their natural instincts.

In addition, be sensitive to the corollary to the attractiveness element, namely your child's desire to fit in. If you introduce your child to lepidoptery (one of renowned author Vladimir Nabokov's lesser known passions), you would be wise to help your child connect with other butterfly collectors. As a practical matter, this should not be difficult because there will always be other children with an interest in one activity or another, be it football, tennis, painting, ballet, reading, or bridge. Do keep in mind though that your child will face pressures to conform, so arm them early with habits that you wish them to maintain during their lives. Consider teaching them to be respectful of others who are not like them.

Based upon your parental wiring, somewhere in your mind are ideas for ways to engage your child in life, to fill their time constructively. Such activities further fill the temporal hole created by raising your child without time-consuming religious activities. I had friends in my childhood years that attended Hebrew school several late afternoons each week, others who spent much of their evening and weekend time at the Mormon Church, and plenty of other friends who dedicated Sundays to Christian Sunday school and related events. They also spent time talking about the religious events they attended, socializing in that environment, and, of course, observing holiday events connected with religion. I think you would agree that with membership in religious institutions comes a certain expectation of time commitment. When I refer therefore to the temporal hole created by raising children without religion, I am referring to the time freed up by avoiding religious commitments of all sorts.

Many parents with whom I have spoken are worried about what to do with their children if they are not spending time involved with these institutions. In most cases, worry not about that. See this as an opportunity, not a problem. But do worry if you are part of a society that in your judgment would harm you or your child if you fail to fit into the religious environment; do what you need to do to protect your family even if that means feigning belief. Please be alert to the possibility that harsh or even violent treatment may await you if you do not at least appear to be religious. Only you can evaluate the risks you face. Even if violence is not likely, you may conclude that failure to at least feign belief would result in too great an economic or societal penalty. While I would encourage you to be courageous in this regard, weighing these complex considerations is your job as a parent, and you must do what is best in your opinion for your family in the face of the realities of your community. I want no martyrs for atheism!

If though you are among the fortunate parents located within communities that afford you the freedom to safely decline to participate in religious activities and to raise your child as you wish, then you may provide your child with the joys and laughter that my kids experienced through a secular upbringing. Think about how to help your child get the most out of life and how to enrich your child. A person is much like a blank canvas awaiting brush strokes of color representing knowledge and experience. Over time and with your guidance, your children may end up with a painting full of color reflecting a full and interesting life.

How one makes use of time is a major issue of life, so the habits and ideas you implant in your child early on will have a large effect upon how your child makes use of time during his or her life. Most of us have no idea what to do with time and I do not profess to have the answer to this riddle, but below is what I perceive as the building blocks of a secular life for a child—the initial strokes of color on the painting representing your child.

Music. From the day they were born, my children heard my singing. (They learned to bear suffering from day one!) Brain wiring begins early and music is an important learning tool for speech, language dexterity generally, and emotional balance. That it is fun, a wonderful bonding opportunity for parent and child, and a life long gift your child can enjoy are other benefits. I found in learning numerous languages that music was extremely helpful in mimicking the complex structures, phraseology, sounds, and vocabulary of languages.

What you sing to your child is up to you. I had a rock band in my youth so I knew a few songs and sang arguably as well as Bob Dylan (to set a low bar at the expense of this gifted Nobel Prize–winning poet), but you need not know songs or sing well to introduce your children to music and enjoy it together. (Of course singing is not the only way to expose your child to music. Teaching them musical instruments is a good idea as well.)

Even at a young age, each of my children had a distinct taste in music, eclectic both as to types of music and the occasion to hear a tune. Through trial and error I learned which melodies would help my baby fall asleep, which would calm a child when upset, which would make them smile, and which they themselves would sing along with me. They rapidly developed an ear for music, sensing chord structure, beat, and harmonies as well as the language differences. Bedtime songs became one of our family rituals, with each child choosing a favorite to hear as he or she drifted off to sleep. If they were crying at bedtime, nine times of out ten, if I just began singing, their tears would slowly fade. While I can only guess about the pleasure they took in hearing this music as infants and toddlers, I can certainly attest to the joy it gave me to sing to them and to watch the effect upon them as we bonded. As they grew, they began singing together or with me, often inventing their own lyrics or melodies.

The songs you sing will be drawn from your culture and of course your personal taste. I sang a selection of typical American nursery tunes ("Bye, baby Bunting," "Rock-a-bye Baby" are examples), but my preference was to sing more popular melodies that I enjoyed myself and that featured interesting harmonies, patterns, chord structures, or words. You can select whatever suits your fancy, but I chose such songs as "Edelweiss," "Feed the Birds," "Katyusha" (Russian), "Lime in the Coconut" (Harry Nilsson), "Guantanamera," "After the Ball" (Irish Ballad), "Goodnight Irene," "Rock Around the Clock," "King of the Road," and "Bottle of Wine" (altering the words of these as I wished), occasionally playing the beat lightly on my child's tummy as we sang together.

While I cannot promise that your children will become multilingual or prolific musicians if you expose them to music (though mine did thanks largely to the efforts of their mom), I would argue that the likelihood of these good things occurring dramatically declines if you fail to do this! But imparting skills and capabilities is only a part of the benefit. The real joy is experiencing the magic of singing together and having this echo through the years. My eldest daughter asked me to sing these childhood songs to her as we drove on I-91 through Springfield, Massachusetts on the way to visit colleges during her junior year of high school. She doesn't remember that now but I sure do! Music establishes lifelong bonds.

How do you deal with religious content in secular music? "Feed the Birds" from *Mary Poppins*, for example, makes reference to saints and apostles. Children who are not exposed to religion do not connect such words with supernatural beings at all. If they ask about the words it is easy to explain that they are imaginary characters not unlike those they see in cartoons. (Of course more detailed explanations should be provided as the children age and hear about religions in school or from classmates.)

As suggested, though, avoiding singing religious songs with your children (though some are pretty) is for the best for the same reason I recommend not reading religious stories to them. After all, this chapter is about how to raise children without religion.

Formal Education. If you want to raise a secular child, do not enroll your child in a school that is affiliated with a religion. Brilliant advice! Then be sure to pay attention to what is happening in the school. I once learned that the headmaster of a secular private school in Manhattan was having all the kids pray for a few moments each day. When I spoke with him, his perspective was that this was fine since the prayer was nondenominational, seemingly unaware that some of us do not believe in any deity at all!

In the United States, our public schools generally do a good job of keeping religion out of schools, though they do often host classroom discussion and activities related to the most politically powerful religious branches in the country, namely Christianity and Judaism, especially around religious holidays. If you live in a country that introduces religion into the school curriculum, then you will have little choice but to discuss religion with your children at an earlier age than might otherwise be necessary if you wish them not to arrive at puberty in a brainwashed state.

Physical Activity. A busy secular life for your child will likely involve sports or some other physical activity. To reduce religious influence upon your child, seek out physical activities that are not associated with churches, synagogues, mosques, etc., but are instead provided by the general community or a public school. As mentioned, this will also lead to the development of friendships for you and your child outside of religious contexts and improve the chances of your child associating with freethinkers.

Books. If you are a parent that encourages your child to read (bravo), then you will also want to exercise diligence when picking reading material. Just avoid religious publications; the rest is easy.

If your children become avid readers, you will have given them a gift that enhances their pleasure in living as well as bolstering their capabilities to achieve material success. Once you find suitable reading material, put your child on your lap and read aloud. Then let your child sound out elementary texts and move on from there. Remember, though, the best way to turn your child into an avid reader is to be one yourself.

Hobbies and Games. I suggest you expose your child at an early age to a broad variety of activities. They can be whatever is available in your area and within your budget. As long as they are not taught in a religious environment, they will fit in well with raising your child without religion. Consider drawing, painting, chess, dance, piano, flute, guitar, sports of all kinds, and family activities that you can do together sometimes.

If you are unable to find a good hobby that clicks with your child, consider introducing them to some with which you might not be personally familiar. The Web site NotSoBoringLife.com offers a list of 308 suggested hobbies.

I found that my kids enjoyed interactive games, particularly those that challenged them to think. For example, after age four, they loved brainteasers of increasing levels of difficulty. On vacations or over meals, I would come up with a brainteaser and let the family ask yes-or-no questions to figure it out. A fun example with which you might be familiar is, "Every morning a man takes the elevator from the 27th floor to the lobby on the way to work, but upon returning goes to the 25th floor and walks up the remaining two flights of stairs. Why?"

What I love about this type of game is that it encourages children to learn what assumptions are and to figure out how to parse through them in a logical manner—to challenge their preconceptions and practice reasoning. If you want to see what I mean by this, have someone in your family find the answer to the above brainteaser online (it is a common riddle, with some variations) and then pose the question to others in the family to see how they break through assumptions and begin to ask better questions. Over time, they will get the hang of it and be ready to progress to tougher challenges. Unlike the game twenty questions, there is not necessarily a limit to the number of questions they may ask, but they all should be answerable with a simple yes or no. While there is more than one possible answer, the actual answer you are leading them toward is by far the most logical, satisfying, and illustrative of the mind's reliance upon assumptions.

Here is a harder challenge that I came up with while on a family vacation in Mexico: The island of Dominica is known for its isolation, scorching sun, and palm trees lining soft, sandy beaches. Last Thursday four intrepid vacationers paddled to the otherwise deserted island where one became the victim of foul play, the body discovered on the beach. Inspector Puree arrived the same day having been summoned by the three suspects. He quickly examined the scene and established definitively that the murder occurred on the beach between noon and 3 pm and that each of the suspects had rock solid alibis for two of those three hours but not for the third hour. Suspect Mr. Green had no alibi between noon and 1 pm, suspect Ms. Rose had no alibi between 1 and 2 pm, and suspect Dr. Black had no alibi between 2 and 3 pm. These facts are undisputed and can be relied upon by you as you formulate questions.

With a flourish, Inspector Puree spun about to his assistant and announced: "I have all the information I need. Tomorrow I will return and tell you which of the three suspects committed this crime." How can he be sure of his ability to identify the murderer?

The answer to this and other riddles cannot be guessed; they must be reasoned out by asking good questions. I imagine I will create some sort of interactive blog so that readers of this book can ask questions about this puzzler!

Chess. Since I play a role in a nonprofit that teaches chess to second and third graders in public schools (over 1.3 million students so far), ran to be the Deputy President of the World Chess Federation, and have witnessed the salutary effects of chess upon young minds in my own family, I would be remiss in not recommending that you introduce chess to your child. It is an inexpensive game (just chess pieces and a board) and costs nothing to learn if you can access the Internet. Chess teaches a child how to plan, calculate, concentrate, organize thoughts, imagine the future, and accept responsibility for mistakes. It teaches strategy, tactics, spatial concepts, geometry, pattern recognition, the value of study and hard work, cause and effect, camaraderie, responsibility, and, in my view most importantly, humility.

Only by playing chess did I learn how difficult it was for me to calculate moves on a 64-square board with 32 pieces with everything right in front of me. How can one not benefit from that humbling experience? The illusion that we are in control and can calculate what will happen in our complex lives dissipates quickly when you blunder and lose a chess game. A sense of modesty and respect for uncertainty replaces the illusion of control and infallibility along with an appreciation for the hard work necessary to accomplish anything in life. These lessons can be learned in other ways but chess covers a broad spectrum of positive skill sets and is fun.

Let me begin by saying that despite its intimidating reputation, chess is relatively easy to learn and fun for children even at an early age. Kids love games and they love to think and compete. My kids began playing with chess pieces as infants and I mean literally playing with the pieces! They picked them up and threw them around while watching others play the game. By age three they were learning some of the rules of the game and were playing by age four. I recall one daughter commenting after I noted that my knight could take her pawn that this would not happen. "Why" I asked? "Because the knight is looking the wrong way." (Knights are horse-shaped figures with eyes. She was making a chess joke.)

If you decide to teach your child chess, the best way is to do it yourself. Your child may only wish to concentrate for a few minutes at first. That is fine. Just keep the experience positive and offer encouragement. Begin at whatever age you like. The current world champion Magnus Carlsen learned at age eight. If you do not know the game, you can go on YouTube and search "learn chess." (There are also numerous excellent books geared to teaching chess to children.) Kids love doing things with their parents, so sitting on your lap learning a game such as chess will thrill them. Just try it once and you will see.

Begin at the end of the game when there are few pieces on the board so the child can learn how the king moves and then how each other piece moves. Show your child basic checkmate structures and pose simple problems. My kids generally preferred solving problems to playing games. The reason not to play full games against a child too soon is that the number of pieces on the board at the beginning of the game creates too much complexity. Instead gradually introduce more pieces and pawns. Be sure to let them experience the joy of "winning" by solving the chess puzzles you provide. This gives you numerous opportunities to compliment them on their concentration, analysis, smarts, etc., which for a child is just the sunlight and water they crave to blossom. I also let them win or draw frequently even after they were old enough to realize I was being nice. They still were happier that way. If your philosophy in this regard is different, you can toughen them up by beating them!

Before you know it, your child will be playing chess with siblings, other youngsters, and grandparents. You will see how proud they are of their accomplishments.

Languages. I wrote earlier about language training and would reiterate that this goes hand in hand with music. Finding ways to teach another language to your child is worthwhile, and unlike, for example, math tutoring, an additional language does not put your child out of sync in school. Language instruction is an excellent use of time during your child's early years, so try to come up with a way to give them the gift of another language.

As mentioned, we picked Mandarin as the third language for our kids. Why? Because it seemed likely that it would be useful to them in light of China's dominant role in the world economy and because we knew our children's minds could handle a complex language at an early age, so we figured we would not "waste" this absorption capability on a language more closely related to English that they could acquire later in life.

If you decide to pick a second or third language for your children, you then need to consider how to teach it to them. As mentioned, including someone in their lives who speaks the language is the best starting point, but it is not required. Let's say you pick Spanish. Here are some steps you can take to teach the language to your baby, starting as early as possible: play infant appropriate music with Spanish lyrics; hire babysitters who speak Spanish; play children's videos on the Internet in Spanish; seek out children in the neighborhood, playgrounds, and schools who speak Spanish to play with your child; and, if you can afford it, retain Spanish-speaking help in your home as a nanny, occasional babysitter, or housekeeper and enroll your youngster in classes conducted in Spanish or in a school that offers a Spanish immersion program.

Reduce Exposure to Television

I humbly suggest that a busy, productive, secular life for your children should not include TV, video games, social media, or apps. (I refer to these sometimes collectively as TV below.) Your children have better things to do with their time. If you fill their early years with substance, you will establish a healthy pattern of learning for them. On the other hand, if your children get used to watching TV, you will establish a very different pattern.

You doubtless realize that in suggesting this path, I may be discussing how your TV habits affect your family, and that is a frightening subject! I realize that many people consider watching

TV alone or with family the best part of the day and cannot imagine living without it, even for the few years necessary to establish healthy habits for your child. If going cold turkey is "inconceivable" to you (to quote the *Princess Bride*, one of my kids' favorite films), then please interpret my points below as arguing for exposing your child to as little TV as possible and doing what you can personally to achieve that.

There are plenty of great reasons to eliminate or reduce TV in your home even if it does run counter to our present TV culture. TV is a relatively new device (just over half a century old) and the verdict is starting to come in that it is harmful for kids. Aggressive behavior, poor school performance, obesity, unhealthy habits including smoking and early sexual activity are all linked to TV.

If you doubt the harmful effects of TV on children and adolescents, consider the American Academy of Pediatrics findings on the matter:

> Although there are potential benefits from viewing some television shows, such as the promotion of positive aspects of social behavior (eg, sharing, manners, and cooperation), many negative health effects also can result. Children and adolescents are particularly vulnerable to the messages conveyed through television, which influence their perceptions and behaviors. Many younger children cannot discriminate between what they see and what is real. Research has shown primary negative health effects on violence and aggressive behavior, sexuality, academic performance, body concept and self-image, nutrition, dieting, and obesity and substance use and abuse patterns. In the scientific literature on media violence, the connection of media violence to real-life aggressive behavior and violence has been substantiated. As much as 10% to 20% of real-life violence may be attributable to media violence. The recently completed 3-year National Television Violence Study found the following: 1) nearly two thirds of all programming contains violence; 2) children's shows contain the most violence; 3) portrayals of

violence are usually glamorized; and 4) perpetrators often go unpunished.

TV exposes your children to words, concepts, and images that you may not wish them to view or hear. While much has been written about violence and sex on TV, we as parents also need to consider less obvious issues, such as how our children are taught to speak and behave. Once you introduce TV to your child, your ability to control these influences diminishes and disappears entirely when you are not present or when your child figures out how to change channels or pressures you to do so!

Think of it this way. You might be okay with a stranger briefly saying hello to your child as you stroll down the street, but how would you feel about that stranger talking with your child for a minute? Five minutes? How about various strangers addressing your child for a few hours each day? That is what happens when your child watches TV. If you pick the programing and closely monitor your child, you will still have little to no control over the abundant advertising content they see. Further, as your child grows, your control will dissipate and this portal to your child will be completely open.

There are additional reasons to avoid TV beyond the deleterious effects on your child. You can save money. TV is after all an advertising delivery system that you pay for. That's right. You pay each month for the pleasure of companies advertising their products to you. If you stop watching TV, you save money by not paying for programing. If your children are not seeing advertising, they will not clamor to buy the latest toy. This saves money and helps make them less materialistic. (I should note that my kids rarely bring up acquiring things, since they are largely shielded from our consumer culture.) Finally, absent TV, you capture massive amounts of time during which you can be more productive and spend more quality time with your children.

I have been pleasantly surprised to find that when I discuss this idea with other parents, many tell me they do not watch TV. There is some evidence that society as a whole may be realizing the life-draining effects of TV. Perhaps we parents can help bring down the viewing time from the stunning five hours a day of TV watching we now average in the United States. The younger generations seem to be leading the way! According to one *New York Times* article, "People 24 and under are watching, roughly, two fewer hours of live TV and DVR programing per week than [in 2015]. And 25-to 34-year-olds (roughly speaking, millennials)? They're watching an hour less per week, down from 27 and a half hours to 26 and a half hours. People between 35 and 49 mostly held steady and are watching about 22 minutes less television per week: 36 and a half hours from nearly 37 hours a week."

While I recommend eliminating TV to parents for all of the reasons discussed, the point about content is of particular importance to parents who wish to limit their child's exposure to religion because programing and commercials contain a great deal of religious content. While you are in a better position than I am to provide examples if you regularly watch TV, what I see on occasion is jarring because my contact with TV is so limited. Recently, as I tuned in while staying at a hotel, commercials came on crammed with religion. They mentioned prayer, the heavens opening up, god, etc.

TV shows and movies glorify religious views and imply that religion is the wellspring of morality, as well as that religious people are somehow better than nonreligious people, and that god, angels, and other religious personifications and embodiments are real. There are myriad examples of this propaganda. As discussed earlier, if you want to raise your children without religion, you should try to avoid exposure to this type of religious promotion until they have developed adequate critical-thinking skills.

There is also often a more subtle issue at work, namely the blurring of reality and religiously imbued fantasy. Consider the movie *Meet Joe Black* about the interaction between an ideal man

(Anthony Hopkins) and the Grim Reaper (a dapper version played by Brad Pitt), who visits Earth in human form to learn what it is to be a human being before "taking" the ideal man to the afterlife. First, let me say that I very much enjoyed this movie. I could not help wondering though how many viewers thought of it as fantasy/science fiction as opposed to dramatizing "real things," such as the Grim Reaper and the process of passage to heaven.

Let's play a game. Real or fantasy? Please answer for each the following: angels, warlocks, goblins, vampires, ghosts, Earth angels, goddesses, hell hounds, the Grim Reaper. The lines are not easy to draw once you step into the realm of believing based on faith. Obviously I see them all as fantasy, but if you are not sure which is which, that doubt is a healthy starting point! How about leprechauns or other "hidden people"? As Michael Lewis noted in *Boomerang: Travels in the New Third World*, excavations in Iceland require approval from governmental experts confirming that the work will not disturb elves. No kidding. This is yet another irrational holdover from an earlier point in human development.

The promotion of religion as well as the blurring of reality and fantasy are among the many reasons why I suggest that you eliminate TV rather than just restrict its access. Half-way measures such as limiting time or channels are difficult to police and create a negative dynamic as you constantly try to micromanage access to the TV. This only makes the TV an object of desire and only works for a while in any event, assuming you are present and ever vigilant. As your children grow older and rightly seek more independence, they will bristle at your attempts to play such a controlling role. The more obvious problem with limiting access (as opposed to totally eliminating it) is that you will not be always present to enforce your TV rules, so your plan will simply not be feasible to implement. Finally, that your children may eventually begin watching TV is no reason not to create good habits for your children while they are young enough to be influenced by your choices.

Even if you agree that you do not want your kids to watch TV, achieving this will be difficult if you watch TV yourself since kids learn by example. For many families, the TV problem accordingly stems from the parents. I am sympathetic! If I have a TV around I have it on, and once it is on, I find it hard to turn off. I attribute this addictive quality to the eye being attracted to movement and ear attracted to sound as well as to our desire for company. The question is whether you can give up having the company of your TV. There is something comforting about watching repetitive news shows, movies, and TV shows with nearly identical plots and endless sports events whose outcome really make no difference to you. I watched *Star Trek* reruns in part because they were familiar.

If you are similar to me in this regard, I suggest you try no TV in your home (or just terminate programing if you cannot physically remove the TV) and rely instead upon the Internet for passive entertainment on an infrequent basis. Your kids will not notice the difference if you start early enough and you will have control over what they see and when they see it. This is certainly practical these days since there are so many entertainment options available on the Internet. You may want to turn on music in your home to help you deal with TV withdrawal.

The worst-case scenario is that you try it, do not like it, and revert to your previous patterns. If you try the experiment, however, you can spend time with your kids (playing, laughing, listening, and teaching) or engaged in work or active recreation. Then, when you wish to watch something, you can pull up a movie on the Internet. My bet is that if you experiment with this dramatic reduction in passive entertainment for six months you will prefer your new life and family dynamic.

My wife is a believer in early-stage home schooling, so she spent time with our children by teaching them math, reading, and writing before they entered kindergarten. We also provided language training by letting them watch cartoons in different languages on the Internet. But how you fill the time will, of course, depend on what you want for your children based on your ambitions, values, and cultural heritage, as well as on what you enjoy doing yourself.

You also might consider using the time previously spent watching TV to invest in yourself (reading a useful book or attending a class), whether to help you earn more money or just to enjoy your life more. (Imagine how our national GNP would skyrocket if we each cut back our TV watching by 50 percent!) After all, the more knowledge you obtain, the more interesting you are to yourself and others as you add more colors to the initially blank white portrait of your life! Alternatively, you can use the time to play a sport, dance, socialize, romanticize, or make babies so you will have more use for this book. There are countless ways to improve your quality of life if you reclaim five hours a day!

If, however, you cannot bring yourself to live without watching TV, try doing so privately to avoid exposing your children to that habit. This is worth a try but will not work as well because your kids will "out" you just as mine "out" me eating ice cream furtively in the evenings while they are supposed to be upstairs bathing for bed. Alternatively, consider well-thought-through restrictions on TV watching and handpick the shows you allow your child to see. Show them some shows and movies that you consider cultural touchstones to link them with their roots or their friends. If you combine this with the steps outlined earlier that create an active life for your child, perhaps your child will have less time for and interest in TV.

In sum, I suggest that you will be a much better parent without a TV in the house. You will be more attentive to your children and a better role model for them. Indeed, you will become a different person around your children without the distraction of TV. Something has to give in order to live life to the fullest extent possible, and cutting the cord to your TV (literally and figuratively) is a simple sacrifice toward that end.

Discipline Your Children Without Religion

Parents often ask me how to discipline children without the "threat" of a god punishing them, but discipline without religion is simple. The typical religious threat—burning in hell—is a bit like using a nuclear weapon to kill a fly. Putting aside that the threat itself introduces irrational thinking (religion) to your children, thereby confusing them and making discipline less clear, it is overkill. Who needs a threat of eternally burning in molten lava to get a child to go to bed on time? Frankly I view such tactics as psychologically abusive. There is no need to terrorize your own child.

In a secular household such threats would be meaningless. So, absent that nuclear weapon, how do you discipline your children? With a little thought, you can provide structure and discipline for your kids without invoking the disapproval of a deity that controls the universe. A tiny fly swatter is more than sufficient.

The first thing to remember is that disciplining youngsters begins with disciplining yourself. If you are able to control yourself, you will have no trouble disciplining your children effectively. If you rarely get angry (admittedly a tall order) and stay relatively detached when your child misbehaves, selecting the right punishment is simple and will generally depend upon your child's age and the severity of the misbehavior. I know this is hard for some people. If you are upset, take a walk or a drive or a break. Do whatever you can to avoid having your bad mood affect your interaction with your child. Being consistently warm toward your children and steady in utilizing discipline on the rare occasions it is needed are key elements of effective parenting.

Children not only need but also want your affection and support. So be absolutely clear up front about the type of behavior you expect from them. Set schedules for the children and keep to them. Offer praise frequently. In other words, discipline begins by setting out proper behavior so your kids know where the lines are. Decide upon your disciplinary steps before they are needed since you will be too emotionally involved to think clearly when you need to employ them.

Do not strike your child EVER (though gently pulling kids apart from one another when they are physically fighting is fine.) There are schools of thought that encourage gentle paddling in extreme cases on the theory that having an object to point to adds control and minimizes the use of corporal punishment. I suggest not doing this because many people have trouble drawing lines once they cross that rubicon of striking a child.

Use time-outs as your primary tactical weapon! Putting a child in the corner or in a separate room is very effective in the early stages of life even if the time span is merely a few seconds. It is your disapproval symbolized by this action that affects the child.

If your children have been fighting (how unusual!) follow the set protocol of identifying the poor behavior, having them apologize—either to you or to whomever they hit—hug, and start playing again. (I almost always have them apologize to each other since both are usually in part at fault.)

When the child is older, slightly longer time-outs are useful. Gentle deprivations of privileges work wonders as they get even older, particularly if you combine them with calm explanations of your family rules and why they are being punished so they will feel fairly treated. Children like all people crave fairness, so use dispute resolution techniques as part of discipline. Ask each child what happened and let each speak. Encourage honesty, sharing, mutual respect, and whatever other values matter to you. How you resolve problems is how they will do so. In time, they will follow your lead and resolve their own disagreements using the methods you showed them.

When you must impose a punishment, stay calm and show regret that you must do this. There is no need to yell, hit, or threaten with eternal damnation! Never forget that you are the main role model, so how you behave will become how they behave. This includes their observations of how you behave in resolving conflicts or when you are upset with them.

Finally, try asking a misbehaving youngster if he or she wants to play as an alternative to discipline when you see a problem developing (the kids begin to push or tease each other). This diffuses the situation and almost always results in a "Yes!" followed by a change in the child's emotional state. Attentive parenting leads to fewer instances arise where discipline is required.

Be a Good Secular Role Model

I hesitate to include the subject of being a role model for morality in a chapter about how to parent without religion, because it implies that parents need not model morality in religious families. They do. Every parent is a role model without necessarily trying to be. If you are conscious of this fact, you are well on your way to being a great parent. Your ethical code will become part of your child's behavioral pattern gradually as your child observes you in countless situations. Your expressions, tone of voice, movements, and actions all signal your child how to behave. The child notices how you treat people and how you talk to them. If you treat everyone with dignity, your child will turn out differently than if you are abusive toward people. Are you honest and courteous in your dealings with others?

I include this discussion though because many people ask how ethical norms are transmitted if not through religion, as if that were a genuine issue. As discussed earlier, religions falsely claim to be the wellspring of morality. They are anything but that. The simple answer is that virtually everyone finds their moral compass in the early years of their lives through their parents.

Over time, that compass is refined further with interactions with other authority figures such as teachers. Your child's friends also have influence over your child. That is why we parents naturally worry about whom our children befriend. So whether a child attends church or a secular community center, his or her moral code will be influenced more by the actions of parents, teachers, and friends than by any message taught from a lectern. Accordingly, I do not believe that children learn (or perhaps better put, observe and absorb) morality from a different source in religious families and nontheist families; in each case the parents are the principal source of moral instruction that over time is supplemented by teachers of all types and by friends.

As discussed earlier, if you choose to welcome strangers into your family via TV, you will need to be alert to the influences that medium provides. While I do not profess to have better ideas than you do about morality, I do wish to note that much of TV programing offers a steady diet of violence, sexual promiscuity, profanity, etc. If you choose to expose your child to that material, discuss with your child whether the behavior they see on TV is proper, particularly as it relates to morality.

So what are some illustrations of how children become moral through their parents' influence? Morality is taught by example. In the early years of a child's life, I respectfully suggest that the word "No" is a key element in teaching children behavior, some of which relates to morality. Parents say this to their young children countless times each day. It is important of course for parents to be consistent in their use of this word to teach effectively and, as the child ages, to back up violations of the word "No" with appropriate discipline.

This process of correction points a child toward the right (morally correct) path, as right and wrong are defined by each parent. Here are some early parenting morality lessons in response to a child's action:

Your baby throws food on the floor while in a high chair learning to eat. "No my love, use your hands to put the tiny pieces of fruit in your mouth."

Your baby pours a training glass full of juice into the eating tray of the high chair. "No dear, that's not how we play."

When your child is a bit older, the lessons are more advanced:

He grabs a cookie before being offered it. "No, honey. Wait your turn. And remember to say, 'Thank you.'"

She hits her brother when he takes her favorite toy. "No, my dear. We don't hit, ever. Ask him to give it back. If he doesn't give it back, come tell me. And you young man, why did you take her toy? Oh, I see, she won't share? Next time ask permission to play with her toy. And you, honey, won't you share with your brother next time? That would make me happy since I love it when you are sweet to each other. Okay, apologize to each other and hug."

As children get older, you will lead them through countless situations involving moral dimensions. For example, you may explain why you recycle bottles and cartons to give children a sense that we are not alone in the world and that we should think about others, or you may explain why we do not waste food, providing some variation of the starving children in India lesson I was taught. Or you may teach them by example as you silently hold the door open for another family and nod to them with a smile.

As they grow even older, your children will observe how you treat servers in a restaurant and how you interact with other drivers on the road. In short, through dozens of daily subtle interactions, your child will observe and absorb much of your ethical framework (your view of right and wrong) just by being around you. Through you they will learn societal norms.

Explain Your Parenting Philosophy to Others

You may find you have little reason to alert the world to your parenting choices, but if you are raising children without religion, there may be times you should tell people. Further, keep in mind that the more parents there are who are open about raising their children without religion, the easier it will be for others to follow suit.

Perhaps the most important scenario in which you will likely need to discuss your secular parenting philosophy with others is if you have parents or other close family members who are religious. Breaking from their religious path may at first cause confusion or discord. You should reassure your family that you are not completely rejecting the family's roots or traditions and certainly are not raising amoral hedonists. Rather, you are taking all of the traditions and teachings (if that is what you plan to do) but leaving out the supernatural element.

Rather than presenting your secular parenting choice as a fait accompli, you may even consider discussing your plans with close family members while you are still determining how best to raise your children to seek their ideas and support. Your parents will already probably know your views about religion. If so, they will not be surprised to learn you are not exposing your kids to it. Once they know your parenting plan, it should not be too difficult to avoid discussing religion (or the lack of it) in front of the children, but depending on your parents' attitudes, you may need to ask them not to engage in religious ceremonies (like praying) when children are present.

A separate subject is how you want to interact during holidays in order to avoid religious themes and the awkwardness of having a disagreement with your parents in front of your kids. The best course is to discuss any concerns with your parents beforehand. I found that this was not difficult since our kids' grandparents respected our decision.

If your parents choose not to cooperate, you should discuss the subject with them privately to reassure them that your children will have a moral upbringing and that you will make efforts to avoid disrespecting them. They likely want the best for their grandchildren, want frequent access to them, and want to avoid conflicts in front of them, so give them opportunities to express their views privately with you. You may need to limit exposure during religious holiday periods to grandparents that wish to force their own beliefs upon your children. If you are careful to show respect to grandparents and avoid attacking their specific religion, most will not put you in the position where you would need to limit contact.

Whether you mention your secular parenting to friends or neighbors depends upon the nature of your relationships and interactions with them, the style of communication you prefer, the type of community you live in, and the character of your individual friends and neighbors. Do they tell you what they are doing with their kids? Usually people just figure out for themselves how neighbors and acquaintances approach religion. Most people are tolerant of different views and welcome the opportunity to teach tolerance to their children, that is, the ability to treat people well without agreeing with all of their opinions and beliefs. You may wish to tell some people what you are doing and why. You may add that you are not teaching your children to be hostile toward religious people.

To explain why you are secular by way of analogy, you might recount Bertrand Russell's concept of a Celestial Teapot.

> Many orthodox people speak as though it were the business of sceptics to disprove received dogmas rather than of dogmatists to prove them. This is, of course, a mistake. If I were to suggest that between the Earth and Mars there is a china teapot revolving about the sun in an elliptical orbit, nobody would be able to disprove my assertion provided I were careful to add that the teapot is too small to be revealed even by our most powerful telescopes. But if I were to go on to say that, since my assertion cannot be disproved, it is an intolerable presumption on the part of human reason to doubt it, I should rightly be thought to be talking nonsense.

CONCLUSION

It may seem harsh for me to try to persuade others about the delusional nature of their religious beliefs and thereby possibly deprive them of the solace and hope that it might provide. Some may say that we should instead support religion to our last breath, either because it is cruel to deprive people of the hope they derive from their religious beliefs, or because they fear that the masses would rise against "us"—were it not for the *in terrorem* effects of religious belief. I have no doubt, with regard to the first point, that religion can provide people with a direction in life and a sense of meaning, self-worth, and purpose, as I have argued. But so can parents, elders, friends, schools, books, and nonreligious civil institutions. Moreover, I believe, with regard to the second point, that it is cynical, exploitative, and tyrannical to perpetuate a falsehood in order to control people, particularly those who are less educated or otherwise vulnerable to religious messages.

Religion requires the suspension of critical rational faculties, if not a suspension of truth itself, in order to impose the deception upon other people and, indeed, upon ourselves. Plato might have regarded it as part and parcel of the noble lie that his philosopher king has to tell in order to control the citizens of the republic after he emerges from the cave. But this lie, noble or not, seems far crueler to me than exposing religion for what it really is. I would rather trust people to figure out for themselves whether religion makes any sense or provides any value to their lives after hearing many different views, than buy into a vague paternalistic concept of offering people false hope to keep them in the dark.

For me, *not* being religious is a source of great strength and comfort. Knowing that we are in this world together, that we have a limited time to live, and that we have only one another to live with is a positive thought. It helps me see this life as real and finite, while simultaneously encouraging me to act sanely and to respect other people. I have no supernatural excuse for thinking or doing otherwise. Similarly, when I see other people suffering, I cannot rationalize it all away by saying that my god wants it that way.

I am hopeful that by rejecting religion other people may be happier seeing it this way too. We know that it is a viable alternative because there are, in fact, many people who already see it this way and find meaning, hope, and solace in their lives without religion.

It is unsettling for religious people to consider the possibility that the millions who have died through the centuries as a result of religious wars have perished without good reason, that most people on the planet spend their lives concerned with issues that are not real, and that the narrative we tell ourselves as a civilization is largely a delusion. But the recognition that we need not continue down this path is a very positive and hopeful thought. Change can indeed occur. One day a major cause of conflict, namely, religion itself, as well as the terrorism it spawns, could simply disappear.

I have enormous respect for anyone who takes care of another person and parents are at the top of that list because they care for children. Whether you are a caregiver, the person who finds a way to make a living everyday to support the caregiver and kids, or some combination of these two roles, you know the strength of character and hard work it takes just to keep everyone clothed, sheltered, and alive. There is no shame in being able to do little more than that.

But if you have the desire and capability to consider the ideas I have shared in this book and to implement some of them, then please do. Moreover, if you find yourself discussing your decision with other parents, consider lending them this book to peruse. It is friendlier than suggesting they buy it.

In the meantime, as we gradually become more civilized, and regardless of where you sit on the spectrum of religiousness (from nontheist to agnostic to doubter to believer to firm believer to fanatic), let's all try to doubt just a little bit more in the infallibility of our beliefs and temper our individual actions accordingly.

Thank you for considering raising your child to be a critical thinker.

APPENDIX

Answers to Common Questions

If you are thinking about raising your children without religion, or are already doing so, you may have some important questions not fully addressed elsewhere in this book. Here, I offer direct answers to some common questions about secular parenting. Please feel free to email me at this book's blog for any other parenting-related questions you might have.

Q: *What is wrong with exposing my kids to religion if only so they can understand what others believe?*

A: There is nothing wrong with teaching your child about various religious views in the world, but put them in a broader context and do so when you teach them about any similarly complex subject, such as Roman mythology. I suggest that you avoid doing it at a young age or suggesting that religious stories are anything more than myths. This will keep them from internalizing these stories as part of their self-narrative.

Q: *What do I tell my kids about their religious grandmother?*

A: Tell them the truth, as always. Explain what grandmother's religious views are about in an age-appropriate manner. Do not disrespect her but do not support her views regarding religion.

Q: *What if they ask more about her religion?*

A: Respond accurately in a manner your child can understand (again, this is largely age dependent). You might note that there are many people who believe in many different religions. If the child asks why you do not believe, you should respond in a truthful manner.

Q: *How will my children react to the knowledge that we are not religious but their grandparents are?*

A: Tell them there is nothing wrong with people having different views. Indeed, that is the spice of life. At the right age you might say to them, "We all love each other and agree on most things, including how wonderful you are, but we do not agree on everything and that is perfectly okay."

Q: *What if my children face taunting at school because they do not believe in any god?*

A: Helping your child deal with harsh treatment by other children is always a difficult and heart-wrenching experience for a parent. We know that our children must face the real world as they emerge from the family cocoon, but we suffer along with our children when that maturation process results in pain to them. Your child may be teased, bullied, and excluded for many "reasons," but typically for not fitting in to some imagined social or cultural standard perfectly. Differences in skin color, hair, clothing, athletic ability, language or style of speech, economic status, social status, religious beliefs, political views, educational level, cultural traditions, food choices, and general social interactive styles all may be called to your child's attention with hostility. By demeaning your child, the bullying child hopes to gain social acceptance or feel superior.

Hugs go a long way in making a child feel better. Then, active listening, and some empathy are largely what they need. But even at an early age I tell my children the truth, that abusive children are insecure and feel bad about themselves. By excluding other children, they create the impression they are part of the in-crowd. (Sound familiar my religious friends?) I teach my children to be good examples for other children, to include the less-gifted athletes or musicians in activities with respect, to not be harsh to children who feel insecurity and act out by creating cliques.

If your child is being singled out for having a secular world-view and understands that is the reason for the criticism, then your child is probably old enough to talk about the subjects covered by this book. School administrators may well help if you bring the matter to their attention.

Q: *What if I lose money for my family by not being part of a religious institution?*

A: If you are poor, you may be receiving money for your family from a church. If you are rich, your referral network may be tied to, for example, a synagogue. It is up to you to decide whether some of those benefits will continue if you raise your kids without religion or whether other doors open when that one closes. Only you can perform the cost-benefit analysis of raising kids without religion. Feigning religious fealty for economic benefit is certainly a common reason why people stay in religious communities, so this choice is yours.

I do not advocate, however, starving your children to

stand for the principle that raising children without religion is the ethical and proper way to raise a family. You must consider practical elements in reaching a decision about your family life and when drawing lines. In many communities, though, you need not raise a banner proclaiming your views and are free to raise your child as you wish.

Q: *How do I deal with the accusation that I have an obligation to expose my children to religion and let them choose for themselves?*

A: First, you have no such obligation. Your obligation is to make the best decisions for your young children that you can and that involves shielding them from harmful influences. Youngsters are not supposed to decide important matters for themselves. If, however, you determine that they are old enough to decide such complex matters for themselves, then do so across the board. There is no such thing as a Christian or Muslim child any more than there is such a thing as a Keynesian or Monetarist child. These are matters of education influencing preferences in thinking. Let your children make the choice of religion when they are old enough to handle similarly complex choices, such as selecting an economic school of thought!

More seriously, though, a practical rule of thumb would be to expose them to religion and allow them to make a choice about it around the time they are old enough to understand the differences between political parties and can make a party choice. But be fair. If you are going to let your children make a choice, then present them with a proper menu of religions, as well as books like this one that argue against religion and in favor of humanism (treating people well because we only have each other). You are not giving much of a choice if you just expose children to your own religion and certainly are giving them no choice at all if you do it when they are very young. That is indoctrination, not choice.

Incidentally, thank those who criticize your decision for their concern. They probably genuinely want the best for your kids. Be kind. Often people are fearful of what they do not understand or are worried they are somehow wrong in what they are doing when they find you are pursuing another path. You might offer them this book and then discuss with them all of the considerations you have weighed in making your decision.

Assuming they decline that offer, you could ask what religious choices they provide to their kids. My bet is you will find they do not mention atheism as a choice and do not undercut their preferred religion by teaching children that there are myriad religions all purporting to be the right one. Rather, the only religion they likely offer is their own religion. Thus, while purporting to promote freedom of choice, what they actually do is provide impressionable young minds with narrow religious indoctrination.

Q: *How do I deal with my kids playing with children who talk about god, heaven, devils, angels, and hell and thus might cause my kids to be frightened and confused?*

A: Young children tend not to have prolonged discussions about philosophy or religious doctrine, so this issue is unlikely to arise until your child is at least six. As always, listen carefully to your child and respond directly. You can remind them that other children are raised differently and then discuss the differences. This can all be done without denigrating other children or other parents who make different parenting decisions than you do.

CHAPTER NOTES

Chapter 1

For a translation of Plato's "Allegory of the Cave," see the Internet Classics Archive, classics.mit.edu/Plato/republic.8.vii.html.

Chapter 2

For a comprehensive list of deities by classification and cultural sphere, see the Wikipedia entry titled "List of Deities," en.wikipedia.org/wiki/Lists_of_deities.

The quote by H. G. Wells comes from his booklet *Crux Ansata: An Indictment of the Roman Catholic Church* (1944).

The quote by Bertrand Russell comes from *The Proposed Roads to Freedom* (1919).

The quote by Karl Popper comes from the chapter "Oracular Philosophy and the Revolt against Reason" in *The Open Society and Its Enemies*, vol. 2 (1945).

The quote by Christopher Hitchens' about religion and death comes from Gregg LaGambina, "Christmas with Christopher Hitchens," *AV Club*, December 20, 2007, www.avclub.com/christmas-with-christopher-hitchens-1798212993.

A number of informative books have been written about the origins of religious belief. Many of them are academic in nature and grounded in a specific discipline, such as anthropology, history, and sociology. For a short, accessible primer on the topic from the perspective of evolutionary psychology, see the book by J. Anderson Thomson, Jr., M.D. (with Clare Aukofer), *Why We Believe in God(s)* (2011).

Chapter 3

The quote by Mark Twain comes from his satirical essay on human nature titled "The Lowest Animal" (1896).

The quote by Thomas Paine comes from *The Age of Reason*, Part I (1794).

The quotes from Sigmund Freud come from his "Thoughts for the Times on War and Death" (1915); *Group Psychology and the Analysis of the Ego* (1921); *The Future of an Illusion* (1927); *Civilization and Its Discontents* (1930); "New Introductory Lectures on Psychoanalysis" (1933); and *Moses and Monotheism* (1939).

For more on Ludwig Feuerbach, see the Stanford Encyclopedia of Philosophy's entry, "Ludwig Andreas Feuerbach," plato.stanford.edu/entries/ludwig-feuerbach/#LateTheoReli

The quotes from Michael Argyle come from his *Psychology and Religion: An Introduction* (2000).

The quote attributed to Michel de Montaigne was quoted by Thomas Jefferson in a letter he wrote to Edmund Randolph dated February 3, 1794.

For the full text of Benjamin Franklin's speech, as recorded by James Madison, see www.pbs.org/benfranklin/pop_finalspeech.html.

Chapter 4

For the fill interview with Frans de Waal, see Kelly Murray, "He Studies Where Morals Come From," CNN, May 16, 2013, www.cnn.com/2013/05/07/health/lifes-work-de-waal/index.html

The quote from Bertrand Russell comes from his introduction in *A History of Western Philosophy* (1945).

The quote that distills Kant's tenet regarding the inadequacy of external pressure on morality comes from professor of anthropology David Kennedy's take on Kant in John Seabrook, "Don't Shoot," *New*

Yorker, June 22, 2009. For more on Kant, see the Stanford Encyclopedia of Philosophy's entry "Immanuel Kant," plato.stanford.edu/entries/kant/.

Chapter 5

The quotation by Richard Dawkins regarding morality comes from Natalie Angier, "The Bush Years; Confessions of a Lonely Atheist," *New York Times Magazine*, January 14, 2001, www.nytimes.com/2001/01/14/magazine/the-bush-years-confessions-of-a-lonely-atheist.html.

The quote from Bertrand Russell comes from his *A History of Western Philosophy* (1945).

The quote by Richard Dawkins about "awed wonder" comes from his book *Unweaving the Rainbow: Science, Delusion and the Appetite for Wonder* (1998).

Richard Dawkins' delivered the Richard Dimbleby Lecture on BBC1 Television on November 12, 1996. A transcript of the lecture, titled "Science, Delusion and the Appetite for Wonder," can be found here: www.edge.org/conversation/richard_dawkins-science-delusion-and-the-appetite-for-wonder.

Chapter 6

If you are looking for a broad discussion of general parenting techniques, you can choose from many books, including two I enjoyed: *Iron John* by Robert Bly (1990) and *King, Warrior, Magician, Lover: Rediscovering the Archetypes of the Mature Masculine* (1991) by Robert Moore and Douglas Gillette.

For a non-Western take on how to raise healthy, happy, multitalented children, see Amy Chua's provocative book, *Battle Hymn of the Tiger Mother*.

The list of hobbies can be found here: www.notsoboringlife.com/list-of-hobbies/.

For the American Academy of Pediatrics study, see Committee on Public Education, "Children, Adolescents, and Television," *Pediatrics* 107, no. 2 (February 2001), pediatrics.aappublications.org/content/107/2/423.

The quote about TV viewing habits comes from John Koblin, "How Much Do We Love TV? Let Us Count the Ways," *New York Times*,

June 30, 2016, www.nytimes.com/2016/07/01/business/media/nielsen-survey-media-viewing.html.

For more on the negative effects of TV, see Joseph Turow, "The Effects of Television on Children: What the Experts Believe," *Communication Research Reports* 2, no. 1 (1985), repository.upenn.edu/cgi/viewcontent. cgi?article=1029&context=asc_papers; Anna Gosline, "Watching TV Harms Kids' Academic Success," *New Scientist*, July 4, 2005, www. newscientist.com/article/dn7626-watching-tv-harms-kids-academic-success/; and "Toddlers and TV: Early Exposure Has Negative and Long-Term Impact," *ScienceDaily*, May 8, 2010, www.sciencedaily.com/releases/2010/05/100503161229.htm.

Two helpful articles with tips on how to avoid parenting mistakes are: Mike Leary, "The 20 Most Common Parenting Mistakes I See," *Fatherly*, January 25, 2016, www.fatherly.com/fatherly-forum/20-common-but-harmful-mistakes-parents-make/ and Melanie Greenberg, "Worst Mistakes Parents Make When Talking to Kids," *Psychology Today*, Mindful Self-Express blog, September 18, 2012, www.psychologytoday. com/blog/the-mindful-self-express/201209/worst-mistakes-parents-make-when-talking-kids.

For a further discussion of societal norms, their role in holding society together, and different perspectives on morality, see *The Righteous Mind* by Jonathan Haidt, in which he discusses how people apply various moral frameworks. For example, liberals tend to value fairness and caring while conservatives tend to value loyalty, authority, and sanctity.

For the full Scalia interview, see Jennifer Senior, "In Conversation: Antonin Scalia," *New York Magazine*, October 6, 2013, nymag.com/news/features/antonin-scalia-2013-10/index3.html.

Russell's teapot analogy comes from an article titled "Is There a God?" which was commissioned, but never published, by *Illustrated* magazine in 1952. For more on Russell's teapot, see Richard Dawkins' take in his TED Talk titled "Militant Atheism," February 2002, www.ted. com/talks/richard_dawkins_on_militant_atheism.

Consider this abbreviated list of films and TV shows that glorify religion and imply religion is the wellspring of morality (in alphabetical order): *Avalokitesvara* (2013); *Barabbas* (1961); *Ben Hur* (1925); *Ben Hur* (1959); *The Bible: In The Beginning* (1966); *The Book of Eli* (2010);

Bruce Almighty (2003); *China Cry* (1990); *Conspiracy of Silence* (2003); *Constantine* (2005); *Courageous* (2011); *Deliver Us from Evil* (2006); *Doubt* (2008); *The Devil's Advocate* (1997); *Elmer Gantry* (1960); *End of Days* (1999); *Escape from Hell* (2001); *Evan Almighty* (2007); *Facing the Giants* (2006); *Fireproof* (2008); *Flywheel* (2003); *Gabriel* (2007); *Ghost Rider* (2007); *Home Run* (2013); *Horns* (2013); *Islam: Empire of Faith* (2000); *Jacob* (1994); *Jacob and Esau* (1963); *Jesus* (1979); *Jesus Christ Superstar* (1973); *Jesus of Nazareth* (1977); *Joan of Arc* (1900, 1928, 1935, 1948, 1999); *Joni* (1979); *Kristo* (1996); *The Last Temptation of Christ* (1988); *Leap of Faith* (1992); *Left Behind: The Movie* (2000); *Left Behind II: Tribulation Force* (2002); *Left Behind: World at War* (2005); *Like Dandelion Dust* (2010); *Lorenzo Ruiz . . . The Saint . . . A Filipino!* (1988); *Marjoe* (1972); *Martin Luther* (1953); *The Night God Screamed* (1971); *Noah* (1998, 2014); *Noelle* (2007); *Old Fashioned* (2015); *One Night with the King* (2006); *Our Fathers* (2005); *The Passion of the Christ* (2004); *Pedro Calungsod: Batang Martir* (2013); *Preacher's Kid* (2010); *Saint Mary* (2007); *Soul Surfer* (2011); *Sunday School Musical* (2008); *The Gospel* (2005); *The Gospel According to St. Matthew* (1964); *The Greatest Story Ever Told* (1965); *The Magdalene Sisters* (2002); *The Hiding Place* (1975); *The Kingdom of Solomon* (2010); *Time Changer* (2002); *Megiddo: The Omega Code 2* (2001); *Faith Like Potatoes* (2006); *The Message* (1976); *The Omega Code* (1999); *The Prince of Egypt* (1998); *A Promise* (2014); *Quo Vadis* (1951); *The Second Chance* (2006); *The Secrets of Jonathan Sperry* (2009); *The Seventh Sign* (1988); *The Song of Bernadette* (1943); *Spartacus* (1960); *The Story of Jacob and Joseph* (1974); *The Ten Commandments* (1923, 1956, 2007); *Unidentified* (2006); *Young Abraham* (2011).

Now consider this small sampling of films and TV shows that blur the line between reality and religiously imbued fantasy (by date): *The Green Pastures* (1936); *Here Comes Mr. Jordan* (1941); *I Married an Angel* (1942); *A Guy Named Joe* (1943); *A Matter of Life and Death* (1946); *Heaven Only Knows* (1947); *The Bishop's Wife* (1947); *For Heaven's Sake* (1950); *Angels in the Outfield* (1951); *The Littlest Angel* (1963); *Heaven Only Knows* (1979); *The Angel* (1982); *The Heavenly Kid* (1985); *Date with an Angel* (1987); *Wings of Desire* (1987); *Earth Angel* (1991); *Faraway, So Close!* (1993); *Angels in the Outfield* (1994); *The Crow* (1994, and its sequels); *Michael* (1996); *The Preacher's Wife* (1996); *Angels in the Endzone* (1997); *Contact* (1997); *A Life Less Ordinary* (1997); *City of Angels* (1998); *Meet Joe Black* (1998); *Dogma* (1999); *The Soul Collector* (1999); *Angels in the Infield* (2000); *Down to Earth* (2001); *Three Days* (TV, 2001); *Wishmaster 3: Beyond the Gates of Hell* (2001); *Constantine* (2005); *Angel-A* (2005); *Gabriel* (2007); *Legion* (2010); *Tensou Sentai Goseiger: Epic on the Movie* (2010); *Tensou Sentai Goseiger vs. Shinkenger: Epic on Ginmaku* (2011); *Gokaiger Goseiger Super Sentai 199 Hero Great Battle* (2011); *Tensou Sentai Goseiger Returns* (2011); *The Littlest Angel* (2011); *I Am Gabriel* (2012); *The Mortal Instruments: City of Bones* (2013); *The Horn Blows at Midnight* (1945); *Dark Angel: The Ascent* (1994); *The Devil's Advocate* (1997); *The End of Evangelion* (1997); *Fallen* (1998); *The Ninth Gate* (1999); *Little Nicky* (2000); *Frailty* (2001); *Ghost Rider* (2007); *A Heavenly Vintage* (2009); *Legion* (2010); *Ghost Rider: Spirit of Vengeance* (2012); *Fallen* (2015).

ABOUT THE AUTHOR

Richard A. Conn, Jr. is an international lawyer and private investment fund manager. He has advised governments on legal restructuring, has delivered a keynote to the United Nations, and is involved in various not-for-profit activities, including one that has taught chess to 1.2 million U.S. public school students. He has four children and lives near New York City.